MW01236347

HOW TO BE A MAN

PURSUING
CHRIST-CENTERED
MASCULINITY

RICK BURGESS & ANDY BLANKS

ARE YOU WILLING TO TAKE THE

HOW TO BE A MAN

CHALLENGE

We've crafted a pretty cool experience to go alongside this book. Now, you can do this book on its own and not miss a thing. But if you'd like to take your experience to the next level, we've created the "How To Be A Man Challenge." The challenge equips you to get the absolute most out of this book.

IF YOU'RE A DAD, THE CHALLENGE WILL HELP YOU AND YOUR SON GROW CLOSER TO CHRIST TOGETHER.

IF YOU ARE A GUY IN A SMALL GROUP WITH OTHER MEN, THE CHALLENGE WILL HELP YOU COLLECTIVELY BECOME THE MEN GOD IS CALLING YOU TO BE.

IF YOU'RE A YOUTH WORKER DISCIPLING TEENAGERS, THE CHALLENGE WILL HELP YOU LEAD THESE GUYS TO PURSUE CHRIST-CENTERED MASCULINITY.

Sure, you can do this without taking the challenge. But don't you want to go bigger? Man up. Take the challenge.

GO TO HOWTOBEAMANCHALLENGE.COM

HOW TO BE A MAN: PURSUING CHRIST-CENTERED MASCULINITY

Published by Iron Hill Press in the United States of America.

ISBN 10: 1935832581
ISBN 13: 9781935832584

Executive Editor
Andy Blanks

Art Director
Laurel-Dawn Berryhill

Graphic Design
Laurel-Dawn Berryhill
Upper Air Creative

Copy Editor
Paige Townley

HOW TO BE

A

MAN

PURSUING
CHRIST-CENTERED
MASCULINITY

RICK BURGESS & ANDY BLANKS

TABLE OF CONTENTS

_____

_____

_____

_____

_____

INTRODUCTION 1

CHARACTERISTIC 1: Identity *(Andy Blanks)* 6

CHARACTERISTIC 2: Integrity *(Rick Burgess)* 18

CHARACTERISTIC 3: Purpose *(Andy Blanks)* 30

CHARACTERISTIC 4: Surrender *(Rick Burgess)* 42

CHARACTERISTIC 5: Passion *(Andy Blanks)* 54

CHARACTERISTIC 6: Commitment *(Rick Burgess)* 66

CHARACTERISTIC 7: Compassion *(Andy Blanks)* 78

CHARACTERISTIC 8: Influence *(Rick Burgess)* 90

CLOSING 102

ABOUT THE AUTHORS 104

INTRODUCTION

Manhood is in crisis in our culture today. Kind of a bleak way to start a book, isn't it? But it's true. In the majority of our churches, men make up the minority of regular attenders. And many of the men who show up on Sunday mornings are disconnected from the work and life of the church.

Did you know that the biblical picture of discipleship in the home is of an active, godly man leading his family? Numerous studies have shown that when a father is obediently following Christ, it's more likely that his family will also be devoted Christians. The only problem with this is that many of our churches don't act like they think this is true. You'll never reach a family by catering programs to women and children in hopes that they would bring the man along with them to church. No, men must be intentionally equipped and discipled. And yet, many of the men we encounter are disconnected from their God-given task of being the spiritual leader of their family.

Why is this? And what can we do about it? These questions have plagued us as we evaluate our own church and the churches and churchgoers we interact with on a regular basis. How can we help men become the men God wants them to be?

What does it even mean to be a man anyway? If you look to today's culture for your answer, you'll have a pretty tough time answering this question.

Searching for a definition of a man in today's world leads to a lot of frus-tration. Everywhere you look there's an example of what not to do. You turn one direction and you see a 20-something (or 30-something) detached from the workforce, spending much of his days playing video games in his mom and dad's basement. Look in another direction and you see a hyper-masculine guy, loud, outspoken, and disdainful of anyone he considers "other." Still, look again and you'll find a guy who resists being "defined" by gender at all, embracing the "anything goes" concept of gender neutrality.

If you want to find examples of how not to be the man God has called you to be, you have plenty of options. All around us are men who are at turns passive, tyrannical, or aimless.

But if you look closer, if you can somehow manage to weed out the imposters, you'll find something refreshing. There are individuals in our communities and in our world who are modeling exactly what it means to be a man. There are guys with blossoming new careers striving to make a difference in their workplace. There are husbands and dads who lovingly and sacrificially lead their wives and children. There are bold but compassionate men all around us who, in the midst of a rapidly changing culture, are shepherding the Church toward a bright future.

So the question is, what do these men know that other guys don't? What's the secret? While there's no way to know for sure (we've talked to a lot of guys, but not all of them), our hunch is that these guys have at least figured out two important things: they're intentionally pursuing manhood, and they're focused on the right ideal.

In essence, these guys have figured out how to be a man.

How do you become a man? First, you have to want to be one. Seems simple, but it's not. There's a very powerful truth our fathers passed on to us, one that we've endeavored to pass on to our children. The truth is this: Most things worth having are only attained through hard work. While this is gloriously untrue about the salvation offered to us by our Heavenly Father, in most other areas of our lives, you have to work for what you want. Want to build a thriving business? You have to work for it. Want to learn a trade? You have to work for it. (You wouldn't want a guy building your house who hasn't worked hard for the experience he's gained.) Want a strong marriage? You guessed it: hard work. Becoming a man is no different.

Most of the guys in this world who fall short of our concept of a real man have one thing in common: They don't want to be

a man. They don't strive to be any better than they are. They don't have a goal. They don't have a vision of what manhood is. And so they are what they are. Think about a guy who you would define as a real man, and chances are he works hard to be the person he is.

How do you become a man? Intentionality is huge. But you can be intentional and still miss the mark. There are plenty of people in this world who work hard at being the man they think they need to be. But the issue is that their model is wrong. They are striving to become the wrong thing.

How do you become a man? It's impossible without grounding your definition of manhood in the person of Christ.

Here's the deal: Through His life, death, and resurrection, Jesus makes it possible for you to have an identity that is completely found in Himself. If you've come to a saving faith in Christ, you're a new creation, having been freed from the bondage of sin. And what you have been freed to become is the man God intends for you to be.

You see, the Gospel perfects masculinity. (It perfects femininity too, but that's a different book . . . one we won't be trying our hands at.) Freed from the chains of sin, given new life and purpose in Christ, and empowered by the very Spirit of God Himself, we are equipped to pursue a masculinity grounded in Christ. Not a masculinity grounded in culture. Not a masculinity grounded in tradition. But a masculinity that looks to Christ as both its source and aim.

Do you want to be a man? Let us tell you how. Actually, let the Apostle Paul tell you how. Though we may be more fun around a campfire, he's undoubtedly better qualified than we are in this area. In Ephesians 5:1-2, Paul says, "Therefore be imitators of God, as beloved children. And walk in love, as Christ loved us and gave himself up for us, a fragrant offering and sacrifice to God." Becoming the man God wants you to be means living like God wants you to live. Imitating God. Walking as Christ walked. Seeing God, especially in the example of Christ, as the pattern for manhood.

How do you become a man? By living like Jesus.

We knew that we wanted to write a book that would help

readers like you pursue a Christ-centered masculinity. We have both been active in ministry for many years. But in the past few years, God has awakened in us a sincere desire to see men – from teenagers to granddaddies – own the identity God has set aside for them. This book is our way of guiding men to understand what they are called to be and challenge them to go after it. But the question was, how? How do we present Christ in such a way that men could see in Him what they are called to be?

We wanted to present Christ as an in-depth model of manhood while simplifying the way in which we understand how to pursue Him. To do this, we identified eight core characteristics we saw in the person of Christ, biblically solid characteristics that we can seek to exemplify in our own lives. These characteristics are powerful ways to view Christ, seeing Him and His actions as expressions of the model man. The characteristics are as follows:

- IDENTITY
- INTEGRITY
- PURPOSE
- SURRENDER
- PASSION
- COMMITMENT
- COMPASSION
- INFLUENCE

The man God has called you to be is a man who knows that his identity and his purpose are completely found in Christ. The man God has called you to be is a man who says what he means and means what he says. His word is always to be counted on. The man God has called you to be is a man who sacrifices for the good of others, first and foremost for the good of his wife and children. The man God has called you to be is a man who wholeheartedly invests himself in life, giving his all to his work and his recreation. The man God has called you to be is a man who uses his influence to

make the world a better place, all in the name of God. This is the man God has called you to be. And brother, it's the man we want you to be as well.

This is simple stuff. And yet, we have to be realistic. Is Jesus more complex than the sum of these eight characteristics? Absolutely. Is it possible to perfectly master these and therefore be the perfect, godly man? Of course not. But these are qualities Jesus modeled and modeled in abundance. And we assure you, with the Spirit's power, if you obediently and passionately pursue Christlikeness by striving to see these characteristics realized in your own life, you will indeed become the man God has called you to be.

It is our prayer that this 40-day devotional will spur you on to a more passionate pursuit of Christ-centered manhood. It's designed to give you manageable devotional content that shouldn't take you more than a few minutes to read, along with questions (what we call "Processing the Pursuit") that will challenge you to apply what you're learning in your life in order to become a real man of God. If this book helps you in that pursuit, we'd love to hear from you. If we can ever help your church or your men's ministry, we'd love to hear from you. If you want to talk about football, hunting, parenting, or life in general, we'd love to hear from you. We're both pretty easy to find.

More than anything, we want you to hear us say that we're men on the same journey you are, striving with humility and effort to grow into Christlikeness every day. We don't always get it right. Neither do you. But we're committed to this journey. And we hope you are too.

Your Brothers in Christ,

Rick Burgess and Andy Blanks

IDENTITY

"Who are you?" It's an interesting question. In fact, it's at the very heart of what it means to be a man. And yet, there are a few ways you could answer this question.

You could respond with your name: "I'm John Smith." And that would say something about you, wouldn't it? That would identify you as John from the family Smith, and depending on your family's legacy, it may say a great deal about your identity. Or it might not really say anything at all.

You could respond to this question with your role. "Who am I? I'm a father. A husband. A brother. A son." While this may speak to more of who you are rather than your name alone, it's still an incomplete way of answering the question.

So maybe you answer the question by listing your hobbies. "Who am I? I'm a runner." Or a handyman. Or a hunter. Or an artist. I play video games. I do CrossFit. I enjoy landscaping. Again, though, this doesn't seem complete. Do we really want to answer the question of who we are by listing the things we do? (For many of us, this is a lot closer to the truth than the other two responses.)

No. None of these responses are complete. None paint the full picture. Who you are is one of the most important questions you can answer. Period. Before you can begin this journey of being the man God has called you to be, you have to know where the starting line is. You wouldn't build a house without laying a good foundation. A solid understanding of our identity is the foundation for pursuing a Christ-centered masculinity. If you have been saved by faith in Christ, then your identity is wonderfully wrapped up in who Christ is. This, before anything else, is the key to understanding how to pursue a life that is God-honoring.

Who are you? The key to answering this question is found in discovering who you are in Christ. The next five days of devotions will help you do just that.

IDENTITY DAY 1

"THEREFORE, IF ANYONE IS IN CHRIST, HE IS A NEW CREATION. THE OLD HAS PASSED AWAY; BEHOLD, THE NEW HAS COME." - 2 CORINTHIANS 5:17

"New" is almost always better than "improved." Given the choice between putting a new transmission in your 2003 SUV or getting a brand new model fresh off the assembly line, what would you choose? A cutting edge laptop is a better choice than an old machine with a new processor. There's usually a pretty big difference between "new" and "improved." This is especially true when it comes to our identities as men.

Read 2 Corinthians 5:17. Here, the Apostle Paul makes a profound statement about the idea of "new" versus "improved." And Paul would know as well as anyone. Paul was the number one enemy of the Church, literally making it his life's mission to persecute Christ-followers. Until Jesus pretty much shut all of that down. As Paul was traveling to Damascus to hunt down more Christians, Jesus appeared to him in a blinding vision and asked Paul why he was persecuting Him. This moment was the line in the sand for Paul, the "point of no return."

The moment we come to a saving faith in Christ, there is death and life. You see, from the moment of his encounter with Christ, Paul's identity was transformed. In his words, the old Paul was dead. And in its place was the new Paul. Did you catch that? Not the improved Paul. Not the better Paul. The NEW Paul. Not Paul 1.1. We're talking Paul 2.0.

To be in Christ is to be made new. The old you that lived in bondage to sin is dead. The old you that lived for you and you alone is dead. The old you that was purposeless is dead. The old you that pursued meaningless things is dead. But the best news is that death is only part of the story.

You see, to understand your identity as a Christ-follower and as a man is to look at the last part of verse 17. "Behold, the new has come." This is the proclamation God makes over you. The same God who spoke creation into existence tells you that you are new. The same God who sent His Son to earth to save His people tells you that you are new. The same God who promises to one day usher in a new order of things where ALL things are made new tells you that you, too, are new. There may be no more empowering promise in Scripture.

Before you can become the man God wants you to be, you must first understand that the man you were is no more. You are new in Christ. And this changes everything.

PROCESSING THE PURSUIT

1. Paul says in his letter to the Romans that if we confess with our mouths that Jesus is Lord and believe in our hearts that God raised Him from the dead, we will be saved from the death our sinfulness rightfully earns for us (Romans 10:9). If we're not careful, the Gospel is something we think of as just "fire insurance." And yet, the Gospel speaks powerfully to our identity in Christ. In your own words, how does the Gospel radically change the way you see yourself and your identity?

2. Sometimes as men, our identity is still tied to "the old," that part of us that is dead. What is keeping you from embracing your identity as a new creation in Christ?

3. Look at the scale below. If 1 represents "a life lived completely for myself," and 10 represents "a life lived completely in Christ," how would you rate the way you're currently living your life? What is your motivation? For whom are you truly living?

1   10

4. Take some time to pray to God right now. Praise Him that He is a God of new beginnings. Thank Him for making you new in Christ. And ask Him to reveal through His Spirit working in you the places in your life where you need to more fully surrender to Him.

IDENTITY DAY 2

"PUT ON THE NEW SELF, WHICH IS BEING RENEWED IN KNOWLEDGE AFTER THE IMAGE OF ITS CREATOR." - COLOSSIANS 3:10

In Colossians 3:1, Paul sets up his argument with a conditional statement. He says, essentially, if you're a Christian, then your focus in life shouldn't be worldly. You should have a Kingdom focus in all you do. This is a HUGE reminder for us as men. But it's only the beginning. Paul then makes a statement in verse 3 that echoes what we studied in yesterday's devotion: The old you has died, and the new you is alive in Christ. Paul goes on to contrast the life of the "dead self" (verses 5-9) versus the life of the "new creation" (verses 12-14). As we seek to pursue a Christ-centered masculinity, this is extremely relevant stuff, and it's where we are going to focus most of our attention today.

In verses 5-9, Paul encourages us to kill the desires in our life that are earthly. Paul rightfully says that these are things that once had a place in our lives, but no longer. These are a dead man's pursuits. If we've come to Christ, we can no longer foster these impulses. It's not a part of our identity as men who are new creations.

So what IS a part of our identity? Paul lists a few examples in verses 12-14. What a stark difference this list is from the previous list! This is a picture of someone who A) has been made new in Christ, and B) is pursuing Christ with all he is worth.

This world tells us much about what it means to be a man, and very little of it is in line with God's character or His ways. What Paul calls us to here is Christ-likeness. Compassion. Kindness. Humility. Patience. Forgiveness. And love. So we must ask, how does this look in your life? What does it mean to be a man who pursues these characteristics?

The attributes Paul lists may not look like the world's definition of being a man, but they are part of God's definition. And seeking to realize them in your life is part of what it means to pursue a Christ-centered masculinity.

PROCESSING THE PURSUIT

1. Think about the list Paul gave us here. Beside each characteristic below, write down what you think it means:

Compassion
Kindness
Humility
Meekness
Patience
Bearing with one another
Forgiving
Loving

2. As a man, which one of these is easiest for you to live out in your life? Circle one or two from the list above that come naturally to you.

3. As a man, which one of these characteristics is more difficult for you to live out in your life? Underline it.

4. For the characteristic you underlined, take a moment and think of three practical examples of how you may live this out today.

5. Here's the cool thing: You're not stuck trying to live out these things on your own. You have the Spirit working within you to make you more like Jesus. But you do have to surrender your will to God. Say a prayer telling God that you want to see Him work in your life to make you more of a man after His own heart. Trust God to finish the work in you that He has started.

IDENTITY DAY 3

"IN THE SAME WAY, LET YOUR LIGHT SHINE BEFORE OTHERS, SO THAT THEY MAY SEE YOUR GOOD WORKS AND GIVE GLORY TO YOUR FATHER WHO IS IN HEAVEN." - MATTHEW 5:16

Read Matthew 5:13-16. These are familiar verses to us. They come just as Jesus is about to kick off His Sermon on the Mount, a large passage of teaching where Jesus flips His audience's religious understanding on its head. Jesus' teaching would have rocked the world of those listening. His goal was to get people to see that while they may have been trying to follow the letter of God's law, they had overlooked the heart of it. He was shaking folks up. And His words should shake us up, too.

These words in Matthew speak to the heart of our identity as men. We were created by God to be difference-makers in this world. Like salt in a bland meal, we are to liven up the world around us for the sake of Christ. Like light, our lives are supposed to dispel the darkness of the fallen world in which we live. Jesus says our lives are literally to be lived in such a way that people observe us and are left to offer praise to God.

Let that last sentence sink in. When people look at your life, does it lead them to look to God? When your children think of you, are their next thoughts of God? When your wife interacts with you, is she led to a deeper pursuit of the Lord? When your co-workers leave your presence, are they left wondering what it is about you that makes you different? Jesus' expectation that you impact your world is intrinsically tied to your identity. It's part of who you are. And yet, so many of us fail to live up to this aspect of our God-given identity.

We have countless opportunities every day to dramatically impact others for Christ, but we are so distracted and so preoccupied that we miss many of them. Awareness of these micro-moments of influence, and the courage to act on them, is the difference between men who make much of their life and men who fail to leave their mark.

As we spend time this week considering our identity in Christ, it's important to grasp what God expects of us. God sees your life as an invaluable resource, a powerful force of influence capable of dramatically impacting the world around you, all for His glory. The question is, do you view your life this way?

PROCESSING THE PURSUIT

1. Consider the areas of influence you have in your life. Where do you have the most influence?

2. How well have you been a steward of your influence? Describe how you have used your influence to bring honor and glory to God.

3. The things you say or don't say have tremendous potential to work as "salt" in our world. Think of a time recently when you said something that made a difference for Christ. Now, think of a time recently when you said (or didn't say) something that was out of character for you. Think about the difference in these two instances. What can you learn from them? How can you be more intentional in how you use your words for God's glory?

4. The identity God has called you to is one of a difference-maker. Spend some time in prayer and reflection today, asking God how He wants to use you as a difference-maker in your world.

IDENTITY DAY 4

"AND HE SAT DOWN AND CALLED THE TWELVE. AND HE SAID TO THEM, 'IF ANYONE WOULD BE FIRST, HE MUST BE LAST OF ALL AND SERVANT OF ALL.'"
- MARK 9:35

Before we finish our look at the foundational concept of our identity, we have to spend some time looking at one of Jesus' core teachings. I think it's one that many of us men, me included, struggle with. It's a teaching that's in stark contrast to the words we sometimes speak to ourselves about what it means to be a man. But it's a concept that is foundational to who Jesus wants us to be.

Read Mark 9:33-37. Capernaum was essentially Jesus' home base. This was where Jesus and the disciples hung out the most. When we encounter Jesus and the guys in Matthew 9, they had been on a kind of walking tour of Galilee and the region to the north. Jesus had been teaching, healing, and performing miracles. Here, we can almost see Jesus seated, relaxed in a house (possibly Peter's), teaching the disciples in a quiet moment.

Look at what Jesus says. He's essentially describing the economy of the King-dom. It's as if He's saying, "Listen up guys, because this is pretty different than how the world sees things." And then He tells them: To be great is to be a servant. To be strong means to be weak. To be first is to be last. What a coun-tercultural message! This is the opposite of our cultural understanding of what it means to be a man, isn't it?

So often in our world, being a man is all about pursuing power and authority. It's crushing the weak. It's being the guy out front or at the top. And yet, this isn't at all how the Bible describes being a man. Jesus says here and elsewhere that greatness in God's eyes is sacrificing for the good of others. It's looking at our spouses, children, employees, friends . . . everyone in our life, and asking, "How can I live in such a way as to always be lifting these people up?"

Servanthood is using your life to make other people's lives better. It's leveraging all of who you are to empower, equip, and encourage those around you. And it's at the very heart of your identity as a Christ-follower.

PROCESSING THE PURSUIT

1. Why is this such a hard concept for us to implement? What is it about seeing ourselves as less than others that seems to strike at the heart of our understanding of masculinity?

2. In Philippians 2:3-4, Paul writes, "[3] Do nothing from selfish ambition or conceit, but in humility count others more significant than yourselves. [4] Let each of you look not only to his own interests, but also to the interests of others." In verse 4, Paul seems to give us a strategy toward actually implementing this concept. What does he say is the key to seeing ourselves as servants?

3. What has to happen in our hearts for us to begin to see the needs of others? What has to happen in your heart for you to be aware of what your wife needs? What has to happen in your heart to truly see what your children need?

4. Take some time today to pray to God. Ask Him to give you a heart of empathy for those around you. Ask Him to give you the discernment to make you aware of what is going on in their lives, as well as courage to act on what He reveals to you. Thank God for serving you by sending His Son to die so that you may have life.

IDENTITY DAY 5

"SO GOD CREATED MAN IN HIS OWN IMAGE, IN THE IMAGE OF GOD HE CREATED HIM; MALE AND FEMALE HE CREATED THEM." - GENESIS 1:27

It's so easy to read these verses in Genesis and breeze right past them without stopping to really reflect on what they mean for us as men. And yet, the statement that God made us in His image should stop us in our tracks. After all, this wasn't said about anything else in God's creation. It was only said about humans. Shouldn't we spend some time thinking about what this means for us and for our identity as men?

What does it mean that we were made in God's image?

Well, it has nothing to do with our physical makeup. God is not a biological person in the way we understand that concept. So being made in God's image must be something other than appearance. I think there are a few ways we can understand this. The first is tied to the second part of verse 26. Being made in God's image means we have dominion, or rule, over creation. We're the apex of creation. We've been given "rule" in a way that no other created thing has been given rule. There are aspects of our worlds that we are in charge, or in command, of. But here's the deal: Our rule was always intended to mirror God's rule! We are to rule with justness, fairness, compassion, humility, and so on. Being made in God's likeness means, in part, being good stewards of anything He has entrusted to us. Our spouses. Our children. His mission. Our very lives.

Second, being made in God's image means we have a shadow of God's nature in us. While we'll never exhibit these traits anywhere near as perfectly or universally as God will, we have the capacity to be loving, forgiving, steadfast, just, and so on. Being made in God's image means that we have the potential to be messengers of godliness in our everyday lives. And so, we have to ask ourselves, how is the world around us better because of God's nature flowing out of us? How are we reflecting God's character in our homes and workplaces? In what ways are our conversations with others ripe for God's nature to transform our world?

Being created in God's image isn't some abstract theological concept. It's a true statement about the nature of our identity as Christ-followers.

PROCESSING THE PURSUIT

1. You have been given "rule," or leadership responsibility, over certain areas in your life. Some of these areas are listed below. Beside each one, briefly describe your rule here. What kind of leader are you in these areas of your life?

Marriage:

Children:

Career:

Church:

2. All leaders have a legacy. How would you describe the legacy you're building for the areas listed above? Are you satisfied with it? If so, what can you do to continue to grow your legacy as a leader? If not, what can you do to change? (There's still time, you know.)

3. Spend some time in prayer today asking God to show you a picture of how you have stewarded the "rule" He has entrusted you with. Ask Him to show you areas in which you have acted in His image by replicating His qualities in your world. Ask Him to reveal to you areas where you need to rely upon Him for improvement.

INTEGRITY

When we think of the word "integrity," we tend to only think about it in terms of telling the truth or not. That's part of it, for sure. But being a man of integrity is so much more than not telling a lie.

When something has integrity, it means that thing is undivided. It is whole. Solid. Intact. Think of the concept of structural integrity in engineering. When a building has structural integrity, it means that it can sustain and support the load for which it was designed. In the technology world, data is said to have integrity when there is no corruption in it. For something to have integrity means that all is as it is intended to be.

When we think about integrity this way, the parallels to our lives quickly become apparent. To have integrity as a man of God is to have all of your life line up with your professed faith. Your thoughts, your actions, your words . . . all of these must reflect a heart that pursues Christ. This is what it means to have integrity.

As we pursue a Christ-centered masculinity, the question of the integrity of our lives is an important one. Are you a man of integrity? The focus of the next five days will help you answer this question.

INTEGRITY DAY I

"LYING LIPS ARE AN ABOMINATION TO THE LORD, BUT THOSE WHO ACT FAITHFULLY ARE HIS DELIGHT." - PROVERBS 12:22

Have you noticed that lying seems to be perfectly acceptable in today's world? As we were working on this book, the 2016 presidential election was in full swing. The detractors of both candidates accused them often (and often loudly) of being liars. Integrity, or the lack thereof, was at the center of the election, which is humorous when you consider that lying seems to be the norm rather than the exception in our culture.

People lie today without concern or consideration for the damage it might cause. The problem with this mentality for a man of God is that the Word of God tells us that Satan himself is the father of lies! In John 8:44, Jesus says that Satan "does not stand in the truth, because there is no truth in him. When he lies, he speaks out of his own character, for he is a liar and the father of lies." Do you hear that?! Jesus Christ says that if you are a liar, you are speaking the language of the devil himself! Notice Jesus doesn't distinguish between a "big" lie and a "little" lie. That kind of hairsplitting is something we came up with. No, Jesus sees only truth and dishonesty. It's pretty clear-cut.

Hear me say this: Dishonesty is very serious. Lying has no place in the life of a man of God. Colossians 3:9 tells us that our integrity is proof of our salvation: "Do not lie to one another, seeing that you have put off the old self with its practices." So let's be clear: if you are a man who claims to be redeemed by the risen Christ, you should not be a man who makes a practice of lying. Bottom line: that belongs to your old self.

When we submit to the authority of Jesus Christ and declare Him Lord of our life, the things that bother God should also bother us. Adrian Rogers once said, "When you are saved by Christ, this doesn't mean you never sin again. But it does mean you are never comfortable with sin again." How comfortable are you with your level of personal integrity?

Examine yourself. Are you a man of integrity? Can you be trusted to tell the truth? Does lying bother you? It should.

PROCESSING THE PURSUIT

1. Are you a man of integrity? Answer that question with a "yes" or "no" in the space below. If you answered "yes," write in one sentence why integrity is so important to you. If you answered "no," write how this makes you feel.

2. Proverbs says that if you are a man of integrity, God takes delight in your faithfulness. Why do you think this is?

3. What impact does your integrity have on your family? How are you leading them to pursue Christ by your example of faithfulness?

INTEGRITY DAY 2

"BETTER IS A POOR MAN WHO WALKS IN HIS INTEGRITY THAN A RICH MAN WHO IS CROOKED IN HIS WAYS." - PROVERBS 28:6

The Book of Proverbs took on a whole new light for me when I realized that it's basically a father instructing his sons in the way a man of God should live. Solomon wrote the majority of Proverbs, and scholars point to two specific settings for Solomon's teachings: in the home, where Solomon is teaching his son (1:8), and in the palace, where a young man is being trained in how to take on the mantle of godly leadership (31:1).[1] In Proverbs 28:6, Solomon is passing along to his sons an important truth: while they may have all the earthly riches in the world, if they lack integrity, then they have nothing.

Solomon is essentially saying that it's better to be poor and have integrity than to be wealthy and have none. Now, there's certainly nothing wrong with being wealthy, nor is there anything evil about being successful. The key is that you must have walked the pathway to success with integrity.

Integrity is of great value in the way we live our lives. Having integrity isn't just a good thing to be able to say about ourselves. It's crucial. Proverbs 4:26-27 says, "Ponder the path of your feet; then all your ways will be sure. Do not swerve to the right or to the left; turn your foot away from evil." As we seek to be the men of God that we are called to be, we are to remain focused on our Lord. He is our path! And Jesus tells us in Matthew 7 that His path is narrow and hard and only a few will find the truth. Acting with integrity may not always be easy, but it's always right.

If you find yourself having any form of success in your life, you have to ask yourself an important question: Did I achieve this His way? Or did I have to compromise my integrity to "get ahead"? If you have compromised God's standard in any way to achieve status, wealth, or success, you would be better off to be poor but to be right with God.

PROCESSING THE PURSUIT

1. If your family was asked whether or not you are a man of integrity, what would they say? How about your friends? Your business partners?

2. What emotions does this last question evoke in you? Did your answer make you feel comfortable about your life? What work do you have to do in this area of your life to get right with God?

3. Can you think of a time in your life when making the right decision cost you financially? Think about that time. Looking back on it, what is the one main thing God taught you through that process?

4. Spend time in prayer today asking God to reveal to you any trouble spots in your life where integrity has been an issue. Allow the Spirit to convict you or to encourage you as needed. Listen to what God is leading you to do as a result.

INTEGRITY DAY 3

"TO DO RIGHTEOUSNESS AND JUSTICE IS MORE ACCEPTABLE TO THE LORD THAN SACRIFICE." - PROVERBS 21:3

Take a second and re-read this verse. Read the proverb and let it resonate. Let your heart marinate on this truth from the Word of God. Here, Solomon is saying that God would rather you live a life of Biblical integrity than make a sacrifice for the Kingdom of God. Our obedience to His Word is of that much value to God Almighty!

As Christians, we have a tendency to downplay obedience. We lean so heavily on God's grace that it's as if we're under the impression that the Bible never calls us to obedience. But that's not the case at all. For example, Jesus says in John 14:15, "If you love me, you will keep my commandments." 1 Samuel 15:22 records the prophet Samuel saying, "Has the LORD as great delight in burnt offerings and sacrifices, as in obeying the voice of the LORD? Behold, to obey is better than sacrifice, and to listen than the fat of rams." To drive home the point, 1 John 2:4-6 says it this way: "Whoever says 'I know him' but does not keep his commandments is a liar, and the truth is not in him, but whoever keeps his word, in him truly the love of God is perfected. By this we may know that we are in him: whoever says he abides in him ought to walk in the same way in which he walked."

This is a really big deal. Jesus says that our obedience is the proof of whether we love Him or not! Any sin that remains in our lives is there simply because we have not arrived to the point that we love Jesus more than we love that sin. A lifestyle of sin is simply a lack of love for Christ.

What does this mean in our lives? It means that if your tithe is right on time every month but you live a life that lacks integrity, that tithe is meaningless before the Lord. If you sacrifice your vacation to go on a mission trip but then return to live a life of disobedience, then the Lord God Almighty just might've preferred that you went to the beach and lived out obedience and integrity as a man of God.

Integrity doesn't earn you salvation, but it's clearly proof of our salvation. What does your lifestyle say about where you stand with God?

PROCESSING THE PURSUIT

1. In Matthew 17, Jesus says that we are known by our "fruit." In other words, people should be able to look at our actions and tell what kind of person we are. What does the "fruit" of your life communicate to others about your faith? Summarize this in one sentence.

2. If we have come to faith in Christ, we are covered by His grace. And thank God for that! If this is true, why do you think Jesus spoke so directly about obedience? Why is it so important that we obey?

3. Making "sacrifices" for our faith can become a form of legalism, can't it? We tend to think we earn points with God any time we put our faith above anything else. But God doesn't work this way. Can you describe a time you did a good thing but your heart wasn't in it?

4. Why do you think God is concerned about our motivation for doing good? Why isn't it enough just to do something positive for God with the wrong motivation?

INTEGRITY DAY 4

"FOR WE AIM AT WHAT IS HONORABLE NOT ONLY IN THE LORD'S SIGHT BUT ALSO IN THE SIGHT OF MAN." - 2 CORINTHIANS 8:21

Have you ever said the following: "I really don't care what people think about me." Well, according to Scripture, you should care quite a bit what other people think.

First, read 2 Corinthians 8:16-21. In this passage, Paul is talking about how he and his companions conducted themselves with integrity while taking up an offering for the Jerusalem church. In this context, verse 21 jumps off the page. Paul knew how important it was that their integrity was above reproach as they carried out their ministry.

The truth that this verse brings to my mind is simply this: We may not always perfectly live out the truth we profess (we're sinners, after all), but the manner in which we live our lives will reveal what we truly believe. Watching the way you and I go about our daily lives - the things we do day-in and day-out - is the truest way to tell what we believe. Our actions will communicate to the world much louder than our words will. Paul knew this, and he was reminding us in verse 21 that our integrity is not only important to the Lord, but also it's crucial in how we communicate the importance of faith to others.

Our actions must line up with our professed beliefs. This is the heart of what it means to be a man of integrity. I was talking with another believer one day who was justifying why he and his child weren't going on a mission trip to a foreign land. The man told me that when his daughter said she wanted to go on the trip, he pointed to a nearby apartment complex and told her that there are plenty of lost people in the complex that need to hear about Jesus. This was absolutely true, so I asked him the following: "So is that what you did? Did you take her to the complex and start knocking on doors?" He looked down at his shoes and had no answer. In that moment, he realized that his actions in this situation didn't line up with his professed beliefs.

The way our lives line up with our words shouldn't confuse people. When we say that we are followers of Christ, our lives should validate this statement. The question you must ask is, does my life validate my profession of faith?

PROCESSING THE PURSUIT

1. You've certainly heard people say, "I don't care what he/she/they think of me." Why is this line of thinking not an option for Christ-followers?

2. How can living a life of integrity bring glory and honor to God in the context in which you do life?

3. Remember, one of our definitions of integrity is the idea of being "undivided," of living a life where your faith impacts everything you do and all that you are. What is keeping you from living a life where your faith in Christ flavors all aspects of who you are as a man?

INTEGRITY DAY 5

"AND THE LORD SAID TO SATAN, 'HAVE YOU CONSIDERED MY SERVANT JOB, THAT THERE IS NONE LIKE HIM ON THE EARTH, A BLAMELESS AND UPRIGHT MAN, WHO FEARS GOD AND TURNS AWAY FROM EVIL? HE STILL HOLDS FAST HIS INTEGRITY, ALTHOUGH YOU INCITED ME AGAINST HIM TO DESTROY HIM WITHOUT REASON.'" - JOB 2:3

We have all heard it said that adversity doesn't create character; it reveals character. Maybe you have experienced great trials in your life. If you have, you know this saying to be true. But when we think about adversity in the Bible, our minds immediately go to Job. And for good reason.

Read Job 2:1-6. Even if you're young in the faith, you most likely have an idea of Job's story. In this well-known passage, we see the beginning of the trials that have afflicted Job. We get a glimpse of this conversation between God and Satan, a situation that, quite honestly, almost defies our understanding of things. Here, God and Satan are talking about Job. God is telling Satan that Job is blameless and upright. And to prove that this is who Job really is, God was going to allow Satan to test Job in order to prove that He was right.

Do you hear that? God will test us to find out if we are the real deal. 1 Peter 1:6-7 tells us that God allows us to experience trials to test the "genuineness of our faith." Proverbs 3:11-12 says that God allows us to face tough times out of His love for us. In other words, Job is simply an example of what God may and likely will do in the life of any man to test that man's integrity. Why? Because God knows that through testing us, He refines our character. Like fire hardens steel, trials strengthen our faith.

Any man who has served in the military or in law enforcement will tell you that maneuvers may train a man for what to look for in battle, but you really don't find out how a man will measure up in combat until someone is shooting back at him with live rounds. So we can read devotions and Scripture all we want, and there is certainly power in that training, but we find out who we really are when our integrity is tested by trials and tribulation in our life.

Our integrity shines brightest in moments of real testing. Your prayer should be that those around you look to you and see that your faith is real when the situation depends on you being able to live what you have learned.

PROCESSING THE PURSUIT

1. What is the greatest trial God has allowed you to experience?

2. What did this trial teach you about God? What did it teach you about yourself?

3. How does this experience inform who you are as a Christian man?

4. Are you in a position where you can thank God for your trials? If so, spend time in prayer to God, thanking Him for allowing you to be tested. Thank Him for staying faithful during your trials and for growing you through adversity. If you're not at a place where you can thank God for your trials, spend time affirming God for who He is and for who He is in your life. Thank Him for His presence. Ask Him to build back up a spirit of trust and assurance in you.

PURPOSE

One of the most important aspects of what it means to be a man is a solid understanding of our God-intended purpose. Without it, we risk spending our time running after the wrong things. And I don't know about you, but I don't have time to waste on things that aren't vital to the mission.

You and I both know men who have struggled with the "why" question.

"Why am I stuck in this job?"
"Why don't I feel like what I'm doing makes much of a difference?"
"Why don't I have a passion for what I'm doing like other men do?"

These questions all point back to one concept: purpose. If we know our purpose and are committed to partnering with the Spirit to see it lived out in our life, we'll be much less likely to struggle with questions about what we're spending our life on. The good news is that the Bible is crystal clear about our purpose. The question we have to ask ourselves is: what does this look like as men to pursue the purpose Christ has called us to?

This week is a focused look at five key areas of your purpose as a man. Our prayer is that after spending time with God in His Word and in prayer that you have a better understanding of your purpose as a man of God and a clear challenge to pursue it.

PURPOSE DAY 1

"ASCRIBE TO THE LORD, O FAMILIES OF THE PEOPLES, ASCRIBE TO THE LORD GLORY AND STRENGTH! ASCRIBE TO THE LORD THE GLORY DUE HIS NAME; BRING AN OFFERING AND COME BEFORE HIM! WORSHIP THE LORD IN THE SPLENDOR OF HOLINESS." - 1 CHRONICLES 16:28-29

Have you ever been outside under a moon so bright it almost felt like daylight? I recall nights in the Marines when we trained under a full moon. Though it wasn't so great from a tactical standpoint, with a full moon at least when you fell in a hole you knew what you were falling into. Now, what does the moon have to do with our purpose as men? Good question. Stay with me . . .

Read 1 Chronicles 16:23-34. David says in verses 28-29, "Ascribe to the LORD glory and strength! Ascribe to the LORD the glory due his name." To "ascribe" a trait to God essentially means that we are to speak back to God, in praise, qualities of His character. Here, David was ascribing to God the glory that God is due because of all the mighty works He has done.

As a man made in God's image, your primary purpose is to live in such a way that your very life "ascribes" glory to God. The way you conduct business, how you lead your family, how you act at the gym or at the deer camp . . . all of these situations are potential opportunities for you to bring glory to God.

Jesus Himself understood that a main aspect of His purpose on earth was to bring glory to the Father (John 17:1-5). And He said that the purpose of our living righteous lives was to bring glory to God, not to us (Matt. 5:16; John 15:8). The psalmist grasped this too: "Not to us, O LORD, not to us, but to your name give glory" (Ps. 115:1). Paul said that no matter what we do, we must "do all to the glory of God" (1 Cor. 10:31). Pretty cool, right?

Now, back to the moon. We know that as radiant as the moon may be at times, it doesn't shine with its own light. It merely reflects the light of the sun. Our lives as men must be lived the same way. Our purpose is to shine not with our own light, but with the reflected light of the Lord. Any good we do, any good thing we have, any positive impact we make . . . everything in our lives should be for the purpose of illuminating the one, true God.

Though it may sustain us in the moment, any glory earned for ourselves is fleeting. Only the glory our lives gain for God is lasting.

PROCESSING THE PURSUIT

1. To glorify God means to bring honor, renown, or great praise to God. It means to bring fame to God, to shine the spotlight on who He is and what He has done. Can you think of some practical ways in which something you have done in the last few weeks has brought glory to God?

2. While there is nothing wrong at all in feeling pride in the things we invest ourselves in or being recognized for our efforts, our natural default as men is to want glory for ourselves. Why do you think this is the case? What need does this type of recognition meet in us? And what's wrong with it?

3. Think about the areas of influence in your life. Do you conduct yourself at work or school in such a way that God is glorified? Do you parent in such a way that God is glorified? Is God glorified in your marriage because of you? Here's a challenge: choose one of these areas and focus this week on being aware of how you glorify God in what you do. Think about where you struggle and where you excel.

4. Spend some meaningful time in prayer to God. Ask Him to give you a big-picture perspective on your life and how you're living it. Ask Him to open your eyes to the opportunities you have to bring Him praise and honor.

PURPOSE DAY 2

"THE LORD GOD TOOK THE MAN AND PUT HIM IN THE GARDEN OF EDEN TO WORK IT AND KEEP IT." - GENESIS 2:15

As we continue to talk about our purpose as men, I want to share a very important statement with you: As a man, part of your purpose on this earth is to work. But your purpose can never be defined by your work. Let me show you what I mean.

Read Genesis 2:1-16. Genesis 2 picks up the creation narrative with a focus on God's creation of man and woman. Pay attention to verses 5-6. Here, the picture of the garden is an incomplete one. They show a garden in need of a gardener. The lack of "small plants" is tied directly to there being no man to work the fields. And so God creates Adam.

In Genesis 2:15 we see that work is part of our inherent identity as men. Before sin corrupted God's perfect creative order, God's plan called for Adam to devote himself to the holy task of working in the garden. Work is part of who we are. Our commitment to our work can be holy and noble. Solomon wrote, "There is nothing better for a person than that he should eat and drink and find enjoyment in his toil" (Eccl. 2:24). But as a result of Adam and Eve's original sin, work was changed for men. We need look no further than God's inclusion of work in part of the pronouncement of judgment against Adam: "By the sweat of your face you shall eat bread, till you return to the ground" (Gen. 3:19). Adam's work ceased to be pure. It became toil. And with this came a corruption of our view of work.

Throughout history, men have developed an unholy relationship with work. The temptation for many men is to find their sole purpose in their job. We become what we do. We devote the best of ourselves to our vocation, leaving precious little for family and faith. Sure, we're called to work hard. Colossians 3:23 says, "Whatever you do, work heartily, as for the Lord and not for men." Proverbs is full of admonitions against laziness. But there's a difference in giving your work your all and giving all of you to your work.

Part of your God-given identity is work. You can't be the man of God you're called to be if you don't work and work hard. But if you're looking for your purpose in your vocation, you're looking in the wrong place.

PROCESSING THE PURSUIT

1. In your own words, describe the level of identity you find in your vocation. Not as you want it to be, but where it actually is. Do you have work to do in how you approach your work?

2. Frustration in our job is the other side of this coin. For some of you, God may be leading you to make a change. If this describes you, what are you waiting for? For others, your frustration in your career might be because you're seeking to find your purpose in your vocation. If this describes you, how can you surrender your frustration to God and seek to have a healthier attitude toward your job?

3. Here's a different angle. God modeled holy work. Look no further than the creation account. God also modeled holy rest: "So God blessed the seventh day and made it holy, because on it God rested from all his work that he had done in creation" (Gen. 2:3). Remember, honoring the Sabbath is one of the Ten Commandments. Do you honor the Sabbath? Do you make time for real rest? If not, why? What message do you send to your family if you aren't obedient in this area?

4. Though it's a challenge for many men, we can find great purpose in our work without having an unhealthy relationship with our vocation. Proverbs 16:3 says, "Commit your work to the LORD, and your plans will be established." Can you think of what this practically looks like for you? How can you commit your work to the Lord in your specific context?

PURPOSE DAY 3

"HUSBANDS, LOVE YOUR WIVES, AS CHRIST LOVED THE CHURCH AND GAVE HIMSELF UP FOR HER." - EPHESIANS 5:25

There can be no discussion of our purpose as men without talking about our role as the spiritual leader of our family. Whether this is something you've struggled with or whether you don't even have a family yet, don't bail out on this devotion. I promise it's worth your time.

The Bible is overflowing with support for the concept of the man as the spiritual leader of his family. Here are just a few verses:
- "But I want you to understand that the head of every man is Christ, the head of a wife is her husband, and the head of Christ is God." - 1 Corinthians 11:3
- "Husbands, love your wives, as Christ loved the church and gave himself up for her." - Ephesians 5:25
- "You shall teach [God's commands] diligently to your children, and shall talk of them when you sit in your house, and when you walk by the way, and when you lie down, and when you rise." - Deuteronomy 6:7
- "Fathers, do not provoke your children to anger, but bring them up in the discipline and instruction of the Lord." - Ephesians 6:4

Men, it's our role to set the spiritual temperature for our home. That is what being the spiritual leader is all about. It doesn't mean that you're the only voice in your home pointing toward the Lord. Remember, a wife is God's perfect provision for a husband. Her voice is needed in the home as much as yours. But the role of the man as the spiritual leader is about initiative. Simply put, your role is to make sure that God's name and ways are alive in your home.

Are you the one who strives to create opportunities for your family to grow closer to the Lord? Are you encouraging your wife in her personal walk with Christ? Are you initiating regular prayer with her? Are you modeling for your kids a Christ-centered love for their mother? Do you look for teachable moments with your children and seize them when the moments arise?

God has put you in your family for a reason. You are the right guy for the job. With the Lord's help, and some intentionality on your part, you can be the leader God has called you to be. What are you waiting for?

PROCESSING THE PURSUIT

1. So, how are you doing on being the guy who sets the "spiritual temperature" for your home? Are there areas in which you're doing OK? What can you do to take your successes here to another level?

2. If you're struggling, what is ONE practical thing you can begin to do to move closer to being the spiritual leader God has called you to be? Think about it, decide on one thing, speak to your spouse about it, and commit to doing it regularly for the next few weeks.

3. Here's the honest to goodness truth: Many men struggle with this because it can feel overwhelming. What if you had a heart-to-heart with your wife? She is God's chosen helpmate for you, after all. And many times our wives have insights that are uniquely different from ours. What if you and your wife came up with a plan together to help you be a more effective leader of your family? Enlist her to pray for you and encourage you. Come up with different roles each of you can play.

4. Spend some meaningful time in prayer today. Ask God to convict you of any deficiencies you have, embolden you and equip you for the task at hand, and lead you as you pursue being a bold yet humble leader in your home.

PURPOSE DAY 4

"BUT YOU WILL RECEIVE POWER WHEN THE HOLY SPIRIT HAS COME UPON YOU, AND YOU WILL BE MY WITNESSES IN JERUSALEM AND IN ALL JUDEA AND SAMARIA, AND TO THE END OF THE EARTH." - ACTS 1:8

We wrote this book during the contentious 2016 presidential election. For many people, neither Hillary Clinton nor Donald Trump was the ideal candidate. Few conservatives considered voting for Clinton, though the fact that some did speaks to how distasteful Trump was to some people. But there were also a number of conservatives who were not fans of Trump and yet voted for him because of how they felt he would lead regarding considerations such as abortion, ISSIS, and so on.

This led to a great deal of public discussion on the Christian's role within society. While there are solid opinions on each side of the issue, the election served as a good reminder for us: God's plan to see culture changed for the sake of the Gospel is people, not policies. As much as we should desire to live in a culture that reflects our morals, God didn't leave the burden of infusing culture with Christian virtues to the government. He left it to us.

Read Acts 1:8. This is Luke's take on Jesus' last words with His disciples before ascending into Heaven. Jesus charged His disciples to take the world-changing message of the Gospel to the ends of the earth. Ever since, Christ-followers have taken up this commission. It is the role of the Church, and the role of men as leaders in the Church, to be people of the Gospel.

But let's focus a moment on the outcome of this commission. We sometimes forget what happens when transformed people live transformed lives. It's contagious! One by one, others are drawn to the Lord through us. Culture can be changed by the passage of the Gospel from person to person. That's the growth plan of the Kingdom.

As a man, one of your primary purposes is to be a messenger of the Gospel. Scripture is as clear about this as it is about anything else. And yet, statistics show that few men invest themselves in sharing the Gospel in the bold, consistent manner in which they are called to do. Don't be one of these men. Be a man who is committed to unfailingly sharing the story of Jesus' life, death, and resurrection. It's who you were made to be.

PROCESSING THE PURSUIT

1. How would others describe your commitment to sharing the Gospel?

2. How do you feel about how you answered that last question? Was it encouraging? Convicting?

3 Where do you have the biggest area of influence when it comes to sharing the Gospel? How can you practically be more effective in communicating the truth of Christ in this specific sphere of influence?

4. Think about your God-given purpose of sharing the Gospel with others. Think about how effective you have been in this area. What do you need to say to God? What work do you need Him to do in your life to make you a more committed communicator of the Gospel?

PURPOSE DAY 5

"AS EACH HAS RECEIVED A GIFT, USE IT TO SERVE ONE ANOTHER, AS GOOD STEWARDS OF GOD'S VARIED GRACE." - 1 PETER 4:10

One of the true honors of my life was meeting the former Commandant of the U.S. Marine Corps, General Louis H. Wilson, Jr. A friend of my wife's grandfather (a great man in his own right and also a former Marine), General Wilson was a recipient of the Congressional Medal of Honor, our nation's highest military honor. General Wilson won the award for his heroic actions in the battle of Fonte Hill in Guam, July 1944.

I would strongly encourage you to go to cmohs.org and spend some time read-ing the descriptions of what these men did to earn the Medal of Honor. Time after time, what you see is that these men risked their life, and sometimes lost it, to save their fellow soldiers and Marines. It notes in General Wilson's cita-tion that despite being badly wounded, "when the enemy launched the first of a series of savage counterattacks lasting all night, he voluntarily rejoined his besieged units and repeatedly exposed himself to the merciless hail of shrap-nel and bullets, dashing 50 yards into the open on one occasion to rescue a wounded marine lying helpless beyond the frontlines." General Wilson under-stood a profound truth about our purpose as men: we're called to sacrificially serve others.

Read 1 Peter 4:10-11. What Peter is doing here is merely backing up what he wit-nessed Jesus teach and model. Peter knew that the man of God sees the gifts and blessings he has been given as a means to serve others. Paul says some-thing similar in Galatians 5:13, that in love we are to "serve one another." And lest we need anymore evidence, Jesus Himself urged us to serve others, saying that He "came not to be served but to serve, and to give his life as a ransom for many" (Matt. 20:28). The Bible is full of examples and exonerations that leave little doubt as to the importance of service as a main part of our purpose.

Hopefully, you'll never be called on to sacrifice your life for the sake of another. But as people trying to be the men of God we're called to be, we should hold on to our lives with a loose hand. Serving others, especially service that costs us, aligns us with Christ. We identify with Jesus when we see other's needs and meet them. Using the gifts you've been given to serve others is a powerful way to fulfill your calling as a godly man.

PROCESSING THE PURSUIT

1. Your family represents what is arguably the most important environment in which to serve. How are you doing here? Are you consistently putting the needs of others in your family above your own?

2. As men, what keeps us from serving others? What are the biggest road-blocks preventing you from giving of yourself to positively impact other people?

3. Throughout the Bible, in literally hundreds of verses and examples, God is seen as having a heart for the less fortunate. What can you do to model God's love for the outcast? How are you giving out of your great abundance of resources to serve those who have little?

4. Make time to spend in prayer with God today. Ask Him to birth in you the heart of a servant. Pray that He would give you opportunities to show His love and mercy to others. And be encouraged by Hebrews 6:10, which says that "God is not unjust so as to overlook your work and the love that you have shown for his name in serving the saints." God will honor your efforts to serve others.

SURRENDER

General George Patton once famously said, "My men don't surrender." He wasn't the only leader who felt this way. Speaking at the height of the Cold War, John F. Kennedy said, "One path we shall never choose is the path of surrender." Shortly before the surrender at Appomattox Courthouse, General Robert E. Lee said he would rather "die a thousand deaths" than surrender to Ulysses S. Grant. One of Winston Churchill's most famous speeches during World War II ended with the admonition to his people, "We shall fight on the beaches, we shall fight on the landing grounds . . . we shall never surrender." Is there anything less manly than surrender?

And yet, at the core of what it means to pursue a Christlike masculinity is a call to surrender. In fact, without truly surrendering your life to Christ, it's impossible to be the man of God you are intended to be. It's that simple.

Jesus modeled this for us, you know. Matthew 26 portrays what is one of the most gut-wrenching moments in Scripture. Here, Jesus pleads with the Father to take away the pain and suffering of the cross. He asks if there is any other way to achieve His mission. But in a moment of powerful surrender, Jesus says, "nevertheless, not as I will, but as you will" (Matt. 26:39). Now that's surrender.

As we will see this week, there is no weakness in surrender. There is no loss. When we surrender to Christ, we gain only strength. We experience only victory. It's a powerful reality that is at the very heart of what it means to be a Christian man. Prepare yourself to be challenged this week to evaluate your level of surrender to Christ.

SURRENDER DAY 1

"SUBMIT YOURSELVES THEREFORE TO GOD. RESIST THE DEVIL, AND HE WILL FLEE FROM YOU." - JAMES 4:7

Years ago, Sherri and I were sitting together in a pastor's office doing a pre-marital counseling session. Little did I know just how radically my life was about to change. As I was sitting across from this pastor, he asked a seemingly innocent question: "Rick, why do you want to get married in this church?" I informed him that the church was centrally located from where my family lived and my future wife's family lived. When he asked me where I attended church, I told him I had no church home, but not to worry because I was a Christian. I reminded him that you don't have to go to church to be a Christian.

The pastor agreed with me from a purely legalistic standpoint. But it was what he said next that blew me away. "Rick, I won't marry you in this church because you're lost." Whoa. I, of course, immediately asked him who he thought he was to make that kind of judgment. I went on to inform him that not only had I believed in Jesus and was baptized when I was a child, but also that when I was a teenager I was baptized again. I'll never forget his reply: "Well you sure can't tell it by the way you live your life."

With those words, the Holy Spirit immediately convicted me. I went home and opened my Bible, something I had not done in 13 years. I was looking for an answer to this question: How could I, a man who "believed" in Jesus, be living a life that was in total conflict with Christ's example? As I opened my Bible, the pages fell to James 4:7: "Submit yourselves therefore to God. Resist the devil, and he will flee from you." As I read this verse, it clicked. The word "submit" jumped off the page. Suddenly I knew the answer to my question.

You see, I had believed in Jesus, but I had never submitted to the lordship of Christ. I was trying to let Him be my Savior without making Him Lord. I was not under His authority. I was attempting to live under my own authority, and my life reflected it. When this painful truth pierced my heart, I literally got on my face in prayer, and in that moment, I surrendered everything to the lordship of Jesus Christ. I was changed forever.

What about you? Are you trying to let Jesus be your Savior without being your Lord? It doesn't work that way. The only right response to Christ is total surrender. Nothing less is acceptable.

PROCESSING THE PURSUIT

1. Why do we fear surrender? What is it about that concept that gives us pause?

2. Scripture makes it clear that we are saved by grace from our sins when we profess faith in Jesus (Eph. 2:8-9). Our good works can't save us. But the Bible is also clear that our actions are proof of our faith (Jas. 2:14-26). What does the nature of your life say to the world about the nature of your faith in God?

3. What are you holding back from God? What area(s) of your life have you not surrendered to Him?

4. The ironic thing about surrender is that we have nothing to surrender. We don't own anything. Technically, our life and everything in it is God's. Surrender is more of a state of mind. It is a posture we take where we look to God and say, "Everything I have is yours." Can you say this to God today? Spend some time in prayer today. Express this sentiment to God. Say it until you mean it. And then listen for what God is telling you to do with the life He has given you.

S U R R E N D E R D A Y 2

"IF ANYONE COMES TO ME AND DOES NOT HATE HIS OWN FATHER AND MOTHER AND WIFE AND CHILDREN AND BROTHERS AND SISTERS, YES, AND EVEN HIS OWN LIFE, HE CANNOT BE MY DISCIPLE." - LUKE 14:26

Today's devotion looks at a powerful interaction found in Luke 14:25-35. Before you read this passage, let's set the stage. This comes in the middle of a long section of Luke's writing where Jesus is making His way to Jerusalem to celebrate Passover. Now, we know that this would be Jesus' last Passover, as His arrest and crucifixion would happen here. Of course, no one in the story outside of Jesus Himself knew that, and so there is great excitement about Jesus and what He is doing.

Now, read Luke 14:25-35. Notice the first sentence: "Now great crowds accompanied him, and he turned and said to them . . ." Great crowds had begun to follow Jesus at this time of His ministry, mainly due to the miracles that He had been doing in order to prove that He truly was the Son of God. But the next sentence began a very tough message on what it will cost anyone who decides to follow Christ.

Even today when we read Jesus' words, we're challenged to the core. "If anyone comes to me and does not hate his own father and mother and wife and children and brothers and sisters, yes, and even his own life, he cannot be my disciple. Whoever does not bear his own cross and come after me cannot be my disciple." Jesus is reminding the crowd, and us to be sure, that we have to count the cost in order to follow Him. For many around the world, counting the cost is extremely real. We know that when a Muslim converts, the entire family opposes them, sometimes to the point of killing them, if they do not renounce Christ. We, too, must ask ourselves if we are willing to go against even our own family if they rebuke Jesus Christ as Lord and Savior.

Our commitment to Jesus must be that strong. Look at verse 33: "So therefore, any one of you who does not renounce all that he has cannot be my disciple." Jesus is telling us here to transfer ownership of our entire lives to Him in order to be a disciple. And so, following Jesus, according to His own words, requires us to (1) count the cost, (2) renounce everything, and (3) transfer ownership of our own lives to Him.

It's one thing to "believe" in Jesus, but as the Scriptures clearly lay out, it's quite another to follow Jesus. It's one thing to talk about what He can do FOR us and quite another to understand what He may require FROM us.

PROCESSING THE PURSUIT

1. Most scholars agree that Jesus' words here about hating one's family is a rhetorical tool called a "hyperbole." It was a common form of Jewish teaching that used overstatements to make a point. It was as if Jesus was saying, "Your love for me must be so strong that your love for anything else should look like hate." How strong is your love for Christ? Do you love Jesus more than anything else in your life? Marinate on this question for a bit. Allow yourself to feel the weight of this question.

2. Much of what Jesus is saying here is about priorities. If you were to literally list in order the priorities of your life, what would that list honestly look like? If you're brave enough, make that list using the space below or a journal.

3. How do you feel about your list? If things are in order, spend some time offering a prayer of thanks to God for leading you to this place. If things are not where you know they need to be, go to the Lord in prayer and ask for both forgiveness and for the Holy Spirit to begin to work a change in your life.

SURRENDER DAY 3

"I HAVE BEEN CRUCIFIED WITH CHRIST. IT IS NO LONGER I WHO LIVE, BUT CHRIST WHO LIVES IN ME. AND THE LIFE I NOW LIVE IN THE FLESH I LIVE BY FAITH IN THE SON OF GOD, WHO LOVED ME AND GAVE HIMSELF FOR ME." - GALATIANS 2:20

So many of us can't mature in our faith because we have yet to be crucified with Christ. We do not want to have the funeral for our old life and truly begin a new life that glorifies God (and removes us completely). If this describes you, let me warn you: Christ loves you enough that He will take you wherever He needs to in order for you to surrender not just your sins, but also your life to Him.

Bronner is the youngest of the five children that God has blessed me to father. And on January 19, 2008, God allowed Bronner to die an earthly death when he drowned in our pool while I was away on a speaking engagement. Notice that I said God allowed Bronner to die an earthly death. Are you OK with that statement? You see, if you don't believe that God allows these things to happen, then you have to believe that God cannot prevent them from happening. Do you serve that God? I don't! And so I know that Bronner's death was something God allowed.

So why did this happen? I could give you many answers to this question, but I will focus on one for this devotion. I recall the first morning I was supposed to return to work after we had laid Bronner's earthly body to rest and held the memorial service. I was alone, sitting in the dark. On that cold winter day, the weight of everything that had happened was so heavy that I couldn't tie my boots. I literally didn't have the strength. And I was supposed to go back to work and present myself to the public and do another radio show? I cried out to God, "How do you expect me to go back and serve you when I can't even tie my boots?!" The answer I received changed my walk with Christ forever.

God's response to me in that moment was crystal clear. He whispered to me in that dark, cold room: "Now you are ready. Your problem has never been that you weren't strong enough. Your problem is that you have never been weak enough. Now you need my help to tie your boots. And now you are ready to be used by me like I have never used you before."

My problem wasn't that I wasn't strong enough. My problem was that I had never been weak enough to be totally dependent on God. I literally needed His strength to tie my boots. I needed His strength to breath! But in that moment, I knew that I had finally been crucified with Christ. I was dead so He could give me life. I was weak. But now He is strong.

PROCESSING THE PURSUIT

1. Strength is an attribute associated with masculinity. It's easy to become physically strong; there are a million gyms across the country that will show you how. Why is spiritual strength so much harder to achieve? In your words, describe the process for developing spiritual strength. What does that look like?

2. In 2 Corinthians, the Apostle Paul wrote that God's power was made perfect in Paul's own weakness, adding, "Therefore I will boast all the more gladly of my weaknesses, so that the power of Christ may rest upon me" (2 Cor. 12:9). What is it about boasting in our weakness that strikes us as un-masculine?

3. The Christian life is full of paradoxes (victory through surrender, greatness through humility, life through death, etc.). What does it practically look like in your life to experience God's strength through owning your own weaknesses?

4. There may be no more important prayer that you can pray as a man than to confess your weaknesses and to truly own their impact on all areas of your life. Only then can you pave the way to truly experience God's strength. Make time to go to God in prayer and own up to how your weaknesses define you. Ask God to show you what it looks like when His strength is your source of power.

SURRENDER DAY 4

"THEN JESUS TOLD HIS DISCIPLES, 'IF ANYONE WOULD COME AFTER ME, LET HIM DENY HIMSELF AND TAKE UP HIS CROSS AND FOLLOW ME. FOR WHO-EVER WOULD SAVE HIS LIFE WILL LOSE IT, BUT WHOEVER LOSES HIS LIFE FOR MY SAKE WILL FIND IT.'" - MATTHEW 16:24-25

Take a moment and read Matthew 16:24-25. You'll recognize some of Jesus' words from the passage we studied from Luke on Day 2 of this week. As we alluded to then, this is a tough truth from Jesus. Why? Because the hardest thing for a fallen, sinful human being to do is to deny one's self.

Everything in our fallen flesh pulls us to gratify ourselves first and foremost, but Jesus makes it clear that in order to truly be a follower of Christ, we must die to ourselves. And the language He uses is powerful. He instructs us to "take up our cross."

Too many times the call for us to "take up our cross" is incorrectly applied. I've heard people refer to an injury or a tough situation as their "cross to bear," but that's not what Jesus is talking about in this challenge. In the time of Roman rule, if you saw someone carrying a cross, they were on their way to die a horrible death. A shameful, painful death reserved for the worst criminals. The call to take up our cross isn't about struggling. It's about dying!

When Jesus Christ tells us to "deny ourselves and take up our cross," He is call-ing us to die to ourselves and let Him live through us. We are to destroy the flesh, which leads to death, and to surrender to the guidance of the Spirit. Our lives are to be pointing people to Him, not us. Romans 8:5-6 says, "For those who live according to the flesh set their minds on the things of the flesh, but those who live according to the Spirit set their minds on the things of the Spirit. For to set the mind on the flesh is death, but to set the mind on the Spirit is life and peace." So in order to live, we must first die to ourselves. We must have a funeral for our flesh.

Are you ready to be a disciple of Christ? If the answer is "yes," then take up your cross, die to yourself, and begin to live for Him.

PROCESSING THE PURSUIT

1. What is the strongest voice of "self" in your life? Is it your career? (Does your work take precedence in your life?) Is it your leisure? (Do you feel like you have a "right" to pursue your hobbies?) Is it a sin habit you struggle with? Or is it just an overarching "me first" attitude that creeps into your daily interactions? Think about this question for a bit. If you were hard pressed to name one area, what would it be?

2. How would your faith be different if you allowed God to put this area of your self to death? How would it change how you serve God? How would it change how He serves others through you?

3. If this is an area of your life that you have seen God work to great effect, what would you say is one of the major differences in how you have come to experience God? How do you know Him better as a result?

4. Putting to death the "self" in all of us is (a) something we cannot do without the Lord's help, and (b) not something we do once and move on. It is an outcome that can only be achieved through the power of God. And it is an action we will have to do over and over again. Spend some time in prayer today. Ask God to begin this work in your life. Ask Him to reveal to you where your "self" is the strongest. Ask Him to give you the power to surrender this part of your life to Him.

S U R R E N D E R   D A Y   5

"BEHOLD, THUS SHALL THE MAN BE BLESSED WHO FEARS THE LORD."
- PSALM 128:4

Take a moment and read Psalm 128:1-4. In verse 1, we see David telling us that the man who fears the Lord and walks in His ways is blessed. This is a great promise. Then, for good measure, David drives the point home again in verse 4 when he says, "Behold, thus shall the man be blessed who fears the Lord."

So what does this really mean to "fear the Lord"? In the original Hebrew, the word that translates into fear is a word that combines "awe" and "dread."[1] So to fear God does literally mean to be afraid of God's ability to bring wrath and destruction in our lives. But it also means to have a deep respect and awe for God that is born out of love for Him. Fearing God means looking at Him as our master or father whom we submit to as our authority. This means we are to be men who take God seriously, not casually. We must live a life like we really believe that God is everywhere (omnipresent) and knows everything (omniscient).

When we are living lives that are a proper sacrifice to our King, we don't bring The Great I Am our leftovers or throwaways. If I wanted to find out if you are the type of man who truly fears God and walks in His ways, I would simply look at your calendar and your bank account. Would I see that God gets your best? Or based on your calendar and bank account would I find that God receives whatever is leftover?

The things we truly care about are the things that we make priorities in our life. If you have not surrendered to the authority of God through faith and experienced the redemption and transformation that only God can bring about in your life, then you likely are not walking in His ways. Until you get to know a King who is benevolent and merciful, you will never have a desire to advance His Kingdom due to the love and thankfulness you have for the gift of mercy and grace.

The reason why so many of us do not consider our salvation to be worth much is because it has never cost us anything. We don't fear God because we don't properly know Him. As you seek to be the man God has called you to be, ask yourself this question: does my everyday life point to my having a proper respect and awe for God?

PROCESSING THE PURSUIT

1. Fear evokes in us a negative reaction. Most all of the things we fear are bad things. Why is the fear of God different?

2. If you don't have a healthy fear of God – that wonderful blend of trembling awe and respect – doesn't it mean that you don't know Him well enough? If this is true, what steps can you take to get to know God better?

3. What is the relationship between a fear of God and a commitment to surrender your life to Him? Can you truly have one without the other?

4. David equates the idea of being blessed with a fear of God. We know God's favor on us is born out of His goodness and isn't fully dependent on our actions (thank goodness). But this is Scripture, so we have to listen to what God is trying to tell us through David. Think on this for a bit: how might we experience more of God's favor through greater surrender to Him? (And the next question would be, "Don't you want this in your own life?")

PASSION

As Rick and I have spent time writing this book and speaking about it in various environments, I've heard him say a phrase about men and women that echoes biblical writers and thinkers: "God made man and woman equal, but He made them different." I love this statement. It is not only true, but also it speaks to the God-given and God-ordained differences between men and women.

Nowhere is this difference more apparent than when it comes to our emotions. While there will always be exceptions on both sides of the argument, it's safe to say that the average man's world is simply not as emotionally saturated as the average woman's. Most men don't have the same emotional filter as women. Sometimes this is a good thing (hence the reason men have about 10% of the relationship drama that women do). Other times our lack of emotional hardwiring is a bad thing; we often miss non-verbal, emotional cues in people or situations that women pick up on immediately. Women trump us (for better or worse) in the feelings department.

But there's a difference between passion and emotion. And while we may not be emotional, if we're going to be the men of God we're called to be, we have to embrace the concept of passionate living.

Now, guys, when I say passion, I don't mean the feelings a man will experience for and with his wife when the kids are spending the weekend at the in-laws. The kind of passion I'm talking about is defined as "a strong liking or desire for or devotion to some activity, object, or concept."[1] It's an approach to life that's deeply stirring or intense. It's the driving feelings or convictions we have about the things that matter to us.

Do you approach your relationship with Christ with passion?
Do you approach your relationships with strong "likings, desires, and devotion"?
Do you serve the Lord with a commitment that is deeply stirring?
Do you have intense feelings about what God has called you to do?

Our goal as men seeking a Christ-centered definition of masculinity is to be able to say "yes" to each of these questions. This week's devotions will help us do just that.

PASSION DAY 1

"THEN I WILL GO TO THE ALTAR OF GOD, TO GOD MY EXCEEDING JOY, AND I WILL PRAISE YOU WITH THE LYRE, O GOD, MY GOD." – PSALM 43:4

Think about someone you love dearly. Do you picture a parent or a sibling? A spouse or a child? A girlfriend or fiancé? A grandparent? If I were to ask you to describe this individual to me, how would you talk about him or her? What words would you use? How would your countenance change as you describe this person?

Hopefully, the way we talk about the people we love is different than the way we talk about other things we love. If you and I were talking about deer hunting or college football, I bet you could tell I enjoy these things. Something about my voice and body language would tip you off. But these are just hobbies. If I were to talk to you about my wife or my kids, I pray that you would be able to tell how much I TRULY love them based on my words, mannerisms, and expressions.

Take a moment and read Psalm 43:4. Look at how David talks about God. He is talking about praising God for helping him out in a bind. Look at what he says: "I will go to the altar of God, to God my exceeding joy." God my exceeding joy . . . what a phrase. The NIV says "my joy and my delight." David pursued God with a great passion, and it shines through in his writing.

Psalm 119 is where David really shows us how his delight for the Lord is at the heart of all he does:
- "I will delight in your statutes; I will not forget your word." – v. 16
- "Your testimonies are my delight; they are my counselors." – v. 24
- "For I find my delight in your commandments, which I love." – v. 47
- "I long for your salvation, O Lord, and your law is my delight." – v. 174

If David chatted you up about the Lord, there would be no doubt about whether he was passionate about God or not. Can the same be said about you?

We can't fake passion. In life, we either care deeply about things or we don't. The same is true about our relationship with God. Either God is your delight or He isn't. The good news is that being passionate about our faith is something we can cultivate. But we have to be committed to it. What's keeping you from passionately pursuing God?

PROCESSING THE PURSUIT

1. If you're married, how did you get to know your spouse? (If you're not married, you can follow the logic here pretty easily.) You invested time and energy into getting to know her. You listened to her. You learned her story. You grew closer to her through shared experiences. You pursued her with passion. Now, ask yourself if your commitment to knowing God looks similar to the commitment you showed in getting to know your spouse. Think about this for a moment.

2. How can you develop a closer relationship with God? List three practical, measurable actions that you can take to begin to pursue God with more of a passion.

3. Spend a few moments in prayer. Ask God to convict you to follow through on these actions. Pray that He will give you the strength and the focus to follow through on pursuing Him with more of a passion.

4. Write down the word "delight" on a notecard or a scrap of paper and put it somewhere you can see it, like the dashboard of your car or on your desk. When you see this word each day, say a silent prayer that God would create in you a delight to follow Him.

PASSION DAY 2

"WHATEVER YOU DO, WORK HEARTILY, AS FOR THE LORD AND NOT FOR MEN, KNOWING THAT FROM THE LORD YOU WILL RECEIVE THE INHERITANCE AS YOUR REWARD. YOU ARE SERVING THE LORD CHRIST." - COLOSSIANS 3:23-24

I have always worked. I was barely 13 years old when I earned my first real paycheck clearing fence lines on Jimmy McGhar's farm. At various times I've sold sunglasses, women's shoes, and mountain bikes. I've had numerous stints in landscaping. I hauled cattle. I built houses. I worked in a top-secret gourmet mushroom factory. I drove dump trucks and bulldozers. I waited tables at a ski resort in Jackson, Wyoming. I worked a half-day at a chicken farm. (The only job I ever quit.) And I still managed to find time to enlist in the Marines.

Work is tied to our identity as men. But today I want to focus on the manner in which we go about our work. I wish I could say that I approached each of the jobs I just listed with passion, but I didn't. There were times in my life when I allowed a dead-end job to impact my passion for work. This was a mistake, as the Bible makes it crystal clear that we are supposed to be men who are passionate about the work we do.

Read Colossians 3:22-24. Here, Paul is speaking directly to a group of people called "bondservants." A bondservant was someone "bound to serve his master for a specific (usually lengthy) period of time, but also as someone who might nevertheless own property, achieve social advancement, and even be released or purchase his freedom."[1] Being a bondservant wasn't the same as being a slave in the way we might tend to think about slavery, but being a bondservant would stink. And yet, let's marvel at what Paul says.

Bondservants were to sincerely obey their masters out of a respect for God and were to be fully committed to their work, working as hard as they would if God were the one giving them their tasks. In doing so, Paul says they ultimately weren't serving their master, but God Himself. Now, let me ask you: if God is concerned with the manner in which a bondservant goes about his or her work, how much more does it apply to you?

Whether you're the president or a plumber, you are called by God to approach the work you do with passion. What does this look like? Being passionate about the work God has you doing is often an internal decision, a commitment of will that says no matter what this day throws at me, I will be diligent in meeting its demands. We embrace this attitude not because we are motivated by approval or advancement, but because we are men seeking to be all that God desires us to be. Do you approach your work with the passion befitting a man of God?

PROCESSING THE PURSUIT

1. Proverbs 13:4 says, "The soul of the sluggard craves and gets nothing, while the soul of the diligent is richly supplied." What do you think it is about passionately pursuing your work that is fulfilling to us as men?

2. Some jobs stink. It's OK to admit it. You may very well be in a job that takes a toll on you. If God is in control of all things, why do you think He is allowing you to be in a tough job? What is it that He is trying to teach you?

3. Many of you reading this are in careers that you find fulfilling. And yet, you may still struggle with approaching your work with passion. What do you need to do to increase your passion for your work?

4. Spend some time in prayer today. Ask God to help you approach your work with passion, no matter the circumstances. Ask the Holy Spirit to show you times when your passion for work has glorified God in the eyes of others.

PASSION DAY 3

"I PRESS ON TOWARD THE GOAL FOR THE PRIZE OF THE UPWARD CALL OF GOD IN CHRIST JESUS." - PHILIPPIANS 3:14

Yesterday we talked about being passionate about our work. Today I want to talk about what it means to be passionate about God's work. As men who are made in the image of God and strive to imitate Him in all we do (Eph. 5:1), we have to be passionate about our role in God's work of redeeming the lost. This is a theme that is covered from several different angles in this book, and yet it's one we can't talk about enough.

Most of us grasp the idea that the Church is God's main way of spreading His story of love, grace, and salvation to a lost world. We know this. But many men don't approach their role in God's plan with much passion. At best, they're inconsistent. At worst, they don't embrace their role at all. The only problem with this is that we're called to be wholly committed to partnering with God in His plan to redeem humankind.

Paul understood this, and his words can be a rallying cry for us. Turn to Philippians 3. Before you read verses 12-17, let me set the context for you. This is Paul near the end of his life. He had been imprisoned in Rome for preaching and teaching the Gospel. The Gospel had cost Paul nearly everything. Paul suffered years of being beaten, ostracized, and verbally abused, all for the Gospel. Finally, he was arrested and imprisoned. Now, read Philippians 3:12-17.

Paul's words here are an amazing encouragement. Paul would have every right to be frustrated with God and disillusioned with His mission. And yet, Paul's words paint a picture of a man who is just as passionate about his role in God's mission as he ever was. He talks about "pressing on" to increase his ownership of his role in God's work. He is able to disregard the frustrations of sharing the Gospel and pour all of his passion into continuing to do the Lord's work. And he finishes this passage by continuing to challenge others to do the same. It's a portrait of a man completely sold out to being used by God.

What would your church look like if you pursued God's work with passion? What would your community look like if all of the men in your church did the same? How would the world be radically impacted if godly men were even half as passionate about God's mission as Paul was? I believe we have the power to change the world for Christ's sake. It starts with passionately embracing our role in God's mission.

PROCESSING THE PURSUIT

1. What is the disconnect between how Paul looked at his role in God's work and how we look at our role? What keeps many men, and maybe even you, from approaching their role in God's work with great passion?

2. As you think about how you have been used by God in the past, can you identify a time when you were super pumped to be doing what you were doing? What was it about that experience that was so meaningful?

3. In his excellent book Wishful Thinking: A Seeker's ABC," Frederick Buechner writes, "The place God calls you to is the place where your deep gladness and the world's deep hunger meet." This quote speaks powerfully to how we can be men who are passionate about our service to the Lord. What makes you deeply glad? Have you ever asked God how you can use the things that make you most glad for the His purposes? Spend some time in thought and prayer over the next few days thinking about how you can take your hobbies, passions, interests, and/or skills and give them to God to use as He will. I promise you from experience, it's the key to unlocking a passion for God's mission.

PASSION DAY 4

"IRON SHARPENS IRON, AND ONE MAN SHARPENS ANOTHER." - PROVERBS 27:17

Do you have men in your life who are really good at being a friend? You know, the guy who, after you've hung out with him, you leave feeling energized? He's the guy who sends you text messages to just check in or to pass along a funny video or joke. He's the guy who's the first one there when something goes wrong. Do you know a guy like this?

What about men in your life who are awesome dads and great husbands? They're the guys who have a healthy level of investment in all areas of their children's lives. They have a great relationship with their wives. And while they aren't perfect, they seem to have an awesome family life. I hope you have men like this in your life. (More than that, I hope you play this role in someone else's life.)

The men that I described above are men who are passionate about the relationships in their lives. Whether it's a friendship or the relationship we have with our family, being passionate about the key relationships in our lives is a concept that flows from Scripture.

- We see a powerful example of friendship between Jonathan and David: "And Jonathan made David swear again by his love for him, for he loved him as he loved his own soul" (1 Sam. 20:17).
- The husband pictured in Proverbs trusts, praises, and encourages his wife (Prov. 31:11, 28-29).
- Proverbs 17:17 says, "A friend loves at all times, and a brother is born for adversity."
- Paul was deeply dedicated to his relationship with Timothy, leading and loving him like a son (1 Tim. 1:2).
- A faithful husband puts his wife's needs and desires ahead of his own (Eph. 5:25).
- Proverbs 18:24 says, "There are 'friends' who destroy each other, but a real friend sticks closer than a brother" (NLT).
- Proverbs 27:17 says, "Iron sharpens iron, and one man sharpens another."
- Jesus modeled the most complete example of someone approaching His relationships with passion in His relationships with His followers, the people He interacted with, and the greater body of humanity He came to save.

These are just a few examples of how the Bible speaks to the passion we're to have toward the relationships that define our lives. As much as anything, the way we approach our relationships is about legacy. How do you want to be remembered? If you're like most men, you want to be remembered as someone who impacted those around you. When it comes to your relationships, being "all in" is the way we model a Christ-centered masculinity.

PROCESSING THE PURSUIT

1. Have you taken a moment to express your appreciation to someone who has been a good friend to you? What's keeping you from firing off a text right now to thank someone who has been a great friend to you?

2. Relationships aren't often (or always) easy. (That's an understatement.) So why is it so important for us to be men who get relationships right? What's at stake if we blow it in this area of our lives?

3. Consider the relationships in your life that matter most. What are three practical things you can do this week to express your passion for these relationships? In other words, what can you do to show the people that matter that you're all in?

4. Do you have a relationship that needs repairing? What's keeping you from initiating the healing that's needed?

5. Spend some time in prayer. Thank God for being in relationship with us and for modeling what a passion for relationships looks like. Ask God to reveal to you actions or attitudes you can embrace that will grow and cultivate your relationships.

PASSION DAY 5

"THE THIEF COMES ONLY TO STEAL AND KILL AND DESTROY. I CAME THAT THEY MAY HAVE LIFE AND HAVE IT ABUNDANTLY." - JOHN 10:10

"One thing this has taught me: I'm going to live each day like it's my last day on earth. I'm going to just appreciate every moment I get." If you've ever encountered someone who has had a close call with death, you may have heard them express a sentiment like this. You may have even said it yourself. What we're essentially saying in these moments is that we want to live a life of passion. There's just one issue: as flawed human beings, everything about who we are inhibits us from ever truly adopting this type of attitude.

Because of how we're wired, it's nearly impossible for us, left to our own best efforts, to pursue each day with passion. We're by nature selfish. Our default is to see life not through a lens of meaning, but a lens of self. We're shortsighted. We have a hard time placing the everyday happenings of our lives into a story that is bigger than we are. And maybe the biggest obstacle is that we're so stinking busy. The pace of our lives makes it a major challenge to stop and appreciate any singular moment. And, yet . . .

Jesus died to free us from the tyranny of our worst self. It's easy to believe that Jesus' life, death, and resurrection only saved us *from* something (sin). But it's vitally important to understand that Jesus came to save us *to* something as well. Jesus came so that we could be saved to approach every day with a passion for living.

In John 10:10 Jesus says, "I came that they may have life and have it abundantly." The life Jesus is talking about here is a life marked by a "rich and unfailing exuberance."[1] Jesus gives "abundance of life and all that sustains life."[2] Because we are sinful, imperfect men, it's easy to dismiss this notion of approaching life with passion. It can seem tangential. It can feel outside of our comfort zone as guys not exactly hard-wired to think about things this way. But it's absolutely vital to grasp how important this teaching is. Jesus is deeply concerned that you have a passion for every day of your life. So much so that He died in order to make it possible.

Are you willing to make the necessary changes in order to pursue your daily life with a Christ-centered passion?

PROCESSING THE PURSUIT

1.It's a cliché, for sure, but we're not guaranteed another moment, yet alone another day. James says our lives are nothing but "a mist that appears for a little time and then vanishes" (Jas. 4:14). And yet, we waste so much of our energy and time on things that don't have eternal value. What in your life robs you of your passion? What can you do to change this? And are you brave enough to do it?

2. Just as Jesus said in John 10:10, an important aspect of His work is that we would experience an "abundant life." Have you ever tried to define what your "abundant life" would look like? What would a life look like where you pursued your work, relationships, ministry, and even your leisure with great passion? Consider taking a few minutes to write down what that might look like.

3. Can you imagine for a moment what would happen if you shaped the course of your life to pursue the vision you just pictured? How dramatically would your existence change if you set in motion a plan to intentionally pursue a passionate commitment in all areas of your life?

4. What's keeping you from being the kind of man Jesus wants you to be and living the kind of life Jesus died for you to live? Ponder this question as you go through your day, and listen for what God is telling you.

COMMITMENT

Each of us can probably name one.

The football coach who has been at the same school for decades.

The older gentleman who has been married to his wife for 50 years.

The greeter who has stood inside your church doors welcoming people for as long as anyone can remember.

What quality unites these men and the many men like them? Commitment.

Commitment is a virtue that is hit-or-miss in our culture today. Men cancel meetings and end marriages alike. We expect people to keep their word, do what they say they will do, or be where they say they will be, only to be disappointed. Many people aren't that committed to the idea of commitment.

Thankfully, there are still many men who are. There are dads who are deeply committed to their kids, husbands committed to their wives, pastors committed to their churches and to the Lord, and so on. And each time men demonstrate strong commitment, they are honoring Christ, who showed us what true commitment looks like.

Consider Christ, who stepped out of heaven to embrace the brokenness of our world. He was mocked, doubted, and ridiculed. God Himself took on the nature of humanity. He knew what it was to be tired and hungry. He experienced pain. And He ultimately died at the hands of the very beings He created. At any given time, Jesus had the power and authority to say "enough is enough." He could have walked away from the grand experiment, and He would have been justified in doing so. But He was unfailingly committed to humanity, and all of creation was changed as a result.

Let this week's focus on commitment challenge you as you strive to be the man of God you were created to be.

COMMITMENT DAY 1

"IF YOU LOVE ME, YOU WILL KEEP MY COMMANDMENTS." - JOHN 14:15

I have always struggled to memorize Scripture. I love the Word of God, and it speaks to me every time I consume it. But for some reason, memorizing every word correctly in a verse or two has always been difficult for me. Today I want us to look at a verse that is very easy to memorize but very difficult to apply in our lives. Read John 14:15-17, paying close attention to verse 15. Here, Jesus essentially says, "If you love me, you'll do what I say." Like I said, easy to memorize, difficult to follow.

We live in a world (and sadly sometimes attend churches) that has cheapened grace to the point that obedience rarely is discussed. The only problem is that the Bible discusses obedience quite a bit, not as anything that earns us salvation, but as the result and proof of salvation. And so what Jesus is doing here is calling us out. Jesus is highlighting a truth we should recognize all too well: many Christ-followers may claim to love Jesus with their mouths, but the way they live tells the truth about their commitment to Him.

I want to pass on a thought that radically changed my walk with Christ: We may not always live what we profess (that's impossible due to our sin-nature), but we undoubtedly live what we believe. Jesus says in John 14 that those who love Him and are with Him obey Him. Those who do not obey Him do not love Him. The bottom line, my brothers, is this: None of us are sin free. It's part of our condition as fallen creatures. But habits or patterns of sin that still remain in your life are there simply because you still love the sin more than you love Jesus Christ. If there is a sin habit that has just become a part of who you are, you're still more committed to sin than you are Jesus. It's a painful truth.

1 John 2:4-5 challenges us to examine our lives when John, inspired by God Almighty, wrote, "Whoever says 'I know him' but does not keep his commandments is a liar, and the truth is not in him, but whoever keeps his word, in him truly the love of God is perfected." Examine your life today. Do you love Jesus more than the sin in your life? If you say you are a follower of Christ, does your life agree with that statement or make you a liar?

PROCESSING THE PURSUIT

1. Do you have a sin habit in your life that you have struggled with for years? If you love Jesus, why are you still holding on to this sin? Don't pass over this question. Let it sink in for a bit.

2. As a man who wants to be more like Christ, what does a commitment to godliness look like for you practically? How do you cultivate it? How do you stay focused on obeying Jesus?

3. Commitment to Christ means putting Jesus above all else. If you have a sin habit in your life that you've not been able to deal with on your own, what's keeping you from enlisting the help of others? If you're serious about being the man God has called you to be, bring your sin habit into the open. Talk about it with someone you trust. Let them help you deal with it.

4. Spend some time in prayer today. Ask for forgiveness from God for the areas in your life where you've consistently struggled with obedience. Ask God to give you the strength to overcome these struggles and become a man more in line with His heart.

COMMITMENT DAY 2

"WHEN THE DAY OF PENTECOST ARRIVED, THEY WERE ALL TOGETHER IN ONE PLACE. AND SUDDENLY THERE CAME FROM HEAVEN A SOUND LIKE A MIGHTY RUSHING WIND, AND IT FILLED THE ENTIRE HOUSE WHERE THEY WERE SITTING." - ACTS 2:1-2

A common mistake we make concerning our walk with Christ is comparing ourselves to the pre-Pentecost disciples. It makes us feel better about ourselves when we see Peter deny Jesus three times after telling Him that he would never forsake Him. Or when the disciples were afraid during the storm. Or when they wouldn't pray with Jesus in the garden because they were tired. At times the disciples' mindset was almost like all they were looking for was a spiritual participation trophy.

The problem with comparing ourselves to the disciples in these moments is that it's all pre-Pentecost, before the Holy Spirit and all of His power was poured out on the disciples (and would from that moment on permanently indwell all who would come to faith in Christ). Suddenly these guys became a much higher standard of comparison.

If we are looking for the standard of how transformed people look, then look to them after Pentecost. The same Peter who denied Christ is now willing to be beaten for speaking about Him. Church tradition tells us that after years of powerful preaching, Andrew was crucified for the Gospel. In fact, the disciples became so committed to advancing the Kingdom of God after Pentecost that besides John, every one of them would eventually be martyred for their faith. And it wasn't just the original disciples who were bold. We see Stephen being stoned to death for his faith. Note that the Holy Spirit was so powerful in his preaching that those who were opposed to Jesus plugged their ears and ground their teeth in anger. Is it any wonder that as he was being stoned, Stephen saw his Lord and Savior Jesus Christ standing at the right hand of God to honor his commitment to the faith?

The example of these men is the standard for you and me! Does this describe you? Would you celebrate being beaten or persecuted for Jesus? The disciples did after Pentecost. No more running. No more cowardice.

In his second letter to Timothy, Paul wrote, "Indeed, all who desire to live a godly life in Christ Jesus will be persecuted" (2 Tim. 3:12). Let me ask you a question: Do you experience persecution? If not, could it be due to your lack of commitment to living a godly life in Christ Jesus? Maybe it's time to reevaluate your level of commitment to living boldly for God.

PROCESSING THE PURSUIT

1. Who is one of the most committed men you know? What are the qualities about this man that you admire most?

2. In what areas of your life have you demonstrated commitment? What do you think is the reason for your successful commitment in these areas?

3. Can you name one or two aspects of your relationship with Christ where your commitment wavers? Now, can you take a moment and identify why you think this is? What are the possible causes of this?

4. What if you made it your aim to be more committed in the areas of your faith in which you struggle? What would that process look like? If you're willing, prayerfully list out what steps you and the Lord might take to begin strengthening your commitment to Him.

COMMITMENT DAY 3

"BEFORE HIM THERE WAS NO KING LIKE HIM, WHO TURNED TO THE LORD WITH ALL HIS HEART AND WITH ALL HIS SOUL AND WITH ALL HIS MIGHT, ACCORDING TO ALL THE LAW OF MOSES, NOR DID ANY LIKE HIM ARISE AFTER HIM." - 2 KINGS 23:25

Look at 2 Kings 23:25. When you first read these words, what king comes to mind? David? Solomon? These words were actually written about King Josiah, a king who ruled hundreds of years after David and is a powerful case study in commitment. Let's go back and look at the steps Josiah made in his life (and in the life of God's people) that earned him this type of accolade.

2 Kings 22 tells us that Josiah did what was right in the eyes of the Lord, walked in the way of David his ancestor, and did not turn aside to the right or to the left. He was committed to God. Now, the first thing Josiah did when he began to reign in Judah was to repair the Temple. In the process, the high priest Hilkiah found the Book of the Law and brought it to the king. When Josiah read God's Word, he was so moved by his sin that he tore his clothes and called for the people to obey the words of this book. So, Step 1 is that Josiah read the Word of God and was so convicted by it that he repented. He began to not only obey the words himself, but also he called on all under his authority to do the same.

In chapter 23, Josiah demanded that all idols be removed from the Temple and the "high places." So brothers, Step 2 in following Josiah's example of commitment is that we must remove anything in our life that is an idol or that blasphemes God. We must also deal with the places in our life that are secret or "off limits" to God and truly vanquish anything we are clinging to that is in conflict or competes with God.

Finally, we see Josiah begin to restore worship in his kingdom. Josiah brought back the Passover to be obedient to God's command to always remember God delivering His people from slavery. Step 3 for us is to remember to look back and celebrate what God has done in our lives.

Josiah took intentional steps to get not only his life properly aligned with God, but also to make sure his entire house was in order under the authority of God. He never moved to the left or the right. He was completely committed, and because he was, he's a powerful example for us as men seeking to be who God has called us to be.

PROCESSING THE PURSUIT

1. Let's spend today processing the steps of commitment Josiah took and apply them in our own lives. Josiah's first step was engaging in God's Word and being moved to repentance by it. What is your level of engagement with God's Word? Are you regularly spending time with God in the Bible? What is your attitude toward the Bible? Is the Bible something that convicts and moves you? We can never be godly men unless we know God, and the Bible is the best way to know Him. Describe how well you are doing with your commitment to the Word. If needed, consider what changes you need to make to get to a healthier level of interaction with God through the Scriptures.

2. Step 2 is easy to spot, but hard to act on. What in your life comes between God and you? Again, easy to spot. If there is something in your life that comes between God and yourself, trust me, you know it. The Spirit has probably already convicted you of it. Do you have something like this in your life? If so, name it. Write it down in the space provided or in a journal. Now, begin today to pray that God would (a) convict you about this, and (b) give you the strength to remove this idol from your life.

3. Step 3 is easy and rewarding. Part of staying committed to God is remembering how He has been committed to you. Make a list of 10 times God has worked in your life. Keep this list in front of you today as a reminder of God's faithfulness.

COMMITMENT DAY 4

"NOT EVERYONE WHO SAYS TO ME, 'LORD, LORD,' WILL ENTER THE KINGDOM OF HEAVEN, BUT THE ONE WHO DOES THE WILL OF MY FATHER WHO IS IN HEAVEN." - MATTHEW 7:21

I remember the first time I heard the words of Jesus Christ speaking in Matthew 7 about those who claim His name but are not with Him. It troubled me to think (incorrectly) that no one really can be sure of their salvation. I have since studied these words many times, and the Holy Spirit revealed to me the part I was missing in this powerful message from our Lord and Savior. It's a gut check for all of us who "say His name."

Read Matthew 7:21-23. Did you catch it? For many years I missed the key phrase in this challenging message to cultural Christians and false teachers everywhere. Jesus says many people declare they are doing things in His name. He then gives us the clue to look for when discerning whether we (or anyone else) are truly with Him. Look carefully. Jesus says, "but the one who does the will of my Father who is in heaven." These are the ones who truly know Him! So if a person is claiming Christ in their lives, their ministry, their business, or their church but are not doing the will of God the Father, they do not know Jesus Christ. Again, doing good works doesn't save us. But our good works reflect a heart that has been transformed by God. More than that, they point to a true commitment to Christ.

In Acts 19, we meet some guys called the Sons of Sceva. These were Jewish exorcists who were jealous of Paul and the miracles that God was doing through him. Not knowing Jesus, they decided they would cast out demons in the name of "Jesus who Paul proclaims." But the demon answered, "Jesus I know, and Paul I recognize, but who are you?" Then the evil spirit jumped on them, beat them, and threw them out of the house half naked. These men used the name above all names to cast out demons, but it did not work. Why? In Paul's hand the name of Jesus had power because he was doing the will of the Father. God didn't honor the efforts of the Sons of Sceva because they had no relationship with Jesus. They didn't know the one behind the name they used.

How about you? Do even the demons recognize your name because of the power of the name of Jesus in your hands?

PROCESSING THE PURSUIT

1. Commitment to Christ can't be faked. You can make lip service to whom you serve, but God knows the nature of your heart. How well does your life testify to your words? Do your actions show a man as committed as his words claim?

2. Look back on your life. In what ways has God honored your commitment to Him? How does thinking about these times help strengthen your faith?

3. The beautiful thing about the Lord is that He is unfailingly committed to us. If you have been saved by grace through faith, you are a new creation. You can be assured of your salvation. God's commitment made in love isn't performance based or conditional. Have you taken a moment and praised God for His commitment to you? Spend the next few minutes in prayer to God. Thank Him for the faithfulness and commitment He has demonstrated in your life.

COMMITMENT DAY 5

"BROTHERS, I DO NOT CONSIDER THAT I HAVE MADE IT MY OWN. BUT ONE THING I DO: FORGETTING WHAT LIES BEHIND AND STRAINING FORWARD TO WHAT LIES AHEAD . . ." - PHILIPPIANS 3:13

As we wrap up our week looking at commitment, I want to spend our last day together talking about the opposite of commitment: apathy. To do this, I want to revisit Philippians 3. Recall that this passage is Paul writing from Rome after being imprisoned for preaching the Gospel. Paul begins by saying that in spite of the amazing work he has done for the Lord, he doesn't think he has "arrived" yet in his commitment to the Gospel. He realizes that if he gets out of jail, he still has much to learn and much yet to accomplish for Jesus Christ.

How about you? Do you consider every day an opportunity to mature in your faith and increase your influence for the Kingdom of God, or have you become apathetic? Are you satisfied with where you are spiritually? Notice what Paul says next about his commitment. He says that he isn't even going to use the time he is imprisoned to reflect on things he has already accomplished. He isn't showing off his trophies. He isn't satisfied with his impact for the Kingdom. After all Paul had done for the sake of God's glory, he writes that he is straining forward to what lies ahead. He wants to do more. He wants to finish strong, reaching for that "well done"!

Is this you, brother? I pray that it is. I pray that you see every day as a chance to make a difference for the Lord. Maybe this describes you. But maybe it doesn't. Maybe you think you've done enough to earn God's favor and now you can knock it out of gear and coast home. I hope this isn't you, but maybe it is.

I want you to hear me say this to you today: if you're guilty of letting up or taking a play off in your willingness to make an impact in God's name, you are simply not properly committed to Jesus Christ. If you look at Scripture for when the heroes of our faith, the men we should look to as our example, stopped advancing the Gospel and maturing in their faith, you won't find it. Until they died, that is.

My prayer for you is that you would be truly and completely committed to advancing the Kingdom and maturing in your faith until you take life's last breath. Anything less is just not enough.

PROCESSING THE PURSUIT

1. What has this week been like for you emotionally and spiritually? Was it a good reminder of staying committed to God? Or was it a kick in the pants? Describe your thoughts, overall, on the concept of commitment in your life.

2. The great thing about our relationship with Christ is that if you're in a bad spot, you don't have to stay where you are. God honors our efforts. If you're reading this book, you're expressing that you want to be a godly man. God will honor that and will lead you toward that goal. Spend some time in prayer today. Ask God to save you from your own worst tendencies. Tell Him that you want to be more committed to Him but that you get in your own way. Pray that He would begin to help you overcome your weakness and that He would give you victories in the small things first, building a foundation of faithfulness in your life. And brother, trust that the work He is doing in you will result in a Christ-centered, faithful life on mission for Him.

COMPASSION

As Rick and I sat down and divided up chapters, I laughed inside when this chapter fell to me. Of the many aspects of Christlike character that I struggle with daily, compassion is definitely one area where I consistently find myself needing to rely on God's grace. I'll admit it . . . I'm not gifted in this area. Maybe you'd admit the same thing.

It's not that I'm not compassionate. It's more that I'm not consistent in my compassion. My heart breaks for those who find themselves dealing with tough circumstances out of their control. I can easily demonstrate compassion to a hurt child, a friend who just got a cancer diagnosis, or an acquaintance who just experienced a tragedy in their family. Someone struggling in his or her sin who doesn't know the Lord? I'm quick with compassion. It comes fairly easy.

You know where I struggle demonstrating compassion? When I've told my child to do the same thing for what feels like the 100th time. Or when my wife and I aren't exactly on the same page. You know where I really struggle? With the person I think should know better. The guy raised in a Christian home who continues to ruin his life with bad decision after bad decision. I have a hard time feeling compassion for that guy.

How eternally grateful I am that Jesus never took this attitude with me.

We're going to spend our time together this week discovering that compassion is at the heart of whom God is, and how, as men striving to live out a Christ-centered masculinity, we must also be men of compassion. It may not come naturally to you. It doesn't to me. But that just makes it all the more worthy of our pursuit.

COMPASSION DAY I

"AS A FATHER SHOWS COMPASSION TO HIS CHILDREN, SO THE LORD SHOWS COMPASSION TO THOSE WHO FEAR HIM." - PSALM 103:13

As we start this week focusing on how we can be men who are more Christ-like in our compassion, let's first carve out some room to see how compassion begins with God. If you begin to look at God through this filter, you will soon realize that compassion is at the very heart of who God is and what His mission is all about. Here are just a few ways we see this expressed in Scripture:

- God's compassion for us is tied to His covenant faithfulness, shown first to the Jews and then, through Christ, to the world (2 Kings 13:23).
- God's compassion for us is never failing (Isa. 54:10).
- Jesus comes to earth as the physical embodiment of God's compassion (Luke 1:72).
- In the Parable of the Prodigal Son, Jesus positioned the father as a metaphor for God Himself. The father is described as running to meet the prodigal. Why? Because "he felt compassion" (Luke 15:20).
- In 2 Corinthians 1:3, Paul writes that God is the "Father of our Lord Jesus Christ, the Father of mercies." The literal Greek translation here is "God is the originator of compassion."[1]

Scripture shows us that God is innately compassionate, and the life and ministry of Jesus is the fullest expression of this. For those made in God's image, seeking to be more Christlike in our expression of our masculinity, compassion has to be a tool in our toolbox. And yet, for many of us, compassion doesn't come easily.

Why? First, we're sinful, and sin starts with self-centeredness. When Jonah got angry at God because He showed compassion on Nineveh (Jonah 4:1-2), it was because Jonah was more concerned with himself than he was with the fate of an entire city. Jonah didn't extend compassion because he was a sinful dude, just like us. Second, most men aren't wired for compassion. It's not something that comes naturally for us. And third, our cultural conception of masculinity doesn't make a ton of room for compassion. We're not compassionate because that would mean we're "soft," and real men aren't soft.

We have to work to overcome these factors. It's easy to say, "I'm just not a guy who's compassionate by nature," and leave it at that. But if we want to be a man after Jesus' heart, we have to be willing to work at it and trust that the Holy Spirit is working alongside us to shape us into the image of God. Let's start that work today.

PROCESSING THE PURSUIT

1. Let's start basic here. Define compassion in your own words. Then, give some examples of what you think it looks like to show Christ-centered compassion to others.

2. Without doing any "research," see if you can list five to 10 instances in the Bible when God and/or Jesus demonstrated compassion to someone.

3. Spend a few moments thinking about times when you have been shown compassion by someone. What impact did that have on your life?

4. Wrap up your time today in prayer. Ask God to show you examples of His compassion at work in the world around you. Seeing Him at work in this way is the start of becoming a man of Christlike compassion.

COMPASSION DAY 2

"PUT ON THEN, AS GOD'S CHOSEN ONES, HOLY AND BELOVED, COM-
PASSIONATE HEARTS, KINDNESS, HUMILITY, MEEKNESS, AND PATIENCE."
– COLOSSIANS 3:12

I loved baseball growing up. I played every sport I could play, but baseball was the most fun to me. I have been a lifelong Red Sox fan, and I can clearly recall in middle school loving the rare chance that the Sox were on national TV. I'd watch Wade Boggs, Mike Greenwell, and Ellis Burks, and then I'd make every attempt to imitate the way they played the game.

Imitation is a big part of how we grow into the men God has called us to be. Christ is our example. We look at Him as a pattern, shifting and forming our thoughts and actions to match His example. Paul understood this and wrote about this concept over and over again. Paul understood that imitating Christ is how we live godly lives (Eph. 5:1-2).

Take a moment and read Colossians 3:5-15. In verse 10, Paul urges his audience to fully live out their new life in Christ, as if they were putting it on like a coat. Then in verses 12-15, he paints a picture of what this new life looks like. Notice that a "compassionate heart" is the first thing Paul mentions as he begins to describe the life we're called to lead. In all of his writings, when Paul calls his audience to act a certain way, he always does so with Christ in view. And so, when Paul urges us to embrace a compassionate heart, he's calling us to have the heart of Christ.

Everything Jesus did for us was born out of compassion, a compassion we never deserved. Mark 6:34 reveals Jesus' mindset upon encountering the mass of people that often followed Him around: "When he went ashore he saw a great crowd, and he had compassion on them, because they were like sheep without a shepherd. And he began to teach them many things." Jesus was will-ing to give up heaven to endure life on this earth so that we might have a way to be in relationship with Him. And all of this was done because He had compassion for us.

When we look at people in our life and, for whatever reason, respond without compassion, we're doing the opposite of imitating Jesus. We're acting like a man who isn't trying to pattern his life after Christ. If we're serious about following Christ, we have to see people and, even if they don't necessarily deserve it, respond the same way Jesus did.

PROCESSING THE PURSUIT

1. If you had to list the three or four biggest barriers to showing compassion to others, what would your list look like?

2. Why do you think Jesus was so compassionate? What was His motivation for responding to people with such compassion?

3. Do you want to be a man who lives out a Christ-centered masculinity? I bet you do. I also bet you want others to see you in a similar light. With this in view, how have you modeled Christ's compassion in the last few weeks or months? Think about ways in which you have responded to people in your life with compassion.

4. Spend time in prayer today. Ask the Holy Spirit to work within you to make your heart more compassionate toward others. Meditate on this idea of imitating Jesus in all you do. Focus on reframing your responses to others in light of being an imitator of Jesus.

COMPASSION DAY 3

"GIVE TO THE ONE WHO BEGS FROM YOU, AND DO NOT REFUSE THE ONE WHO WOULD BORROW FROM YOU." – MATTHEW 5:42

I was standing in the Target parking lot when she approached me. She was a middle-aged woman, disheveled and crying. She launched into a hard-luck story and hadn't made it far when I interrupted her to ask how I could help. She said she needed money for groceries for her children and herself. I told her that I didn't have any cash, but that if she wanted, we could go back inside and I would buy her some groceries. She said that would be great, and so in we went. We chatted briefly, if not awkwardly, as we walked up and down the aisles.

We went through the checkout line together where I gladly paid for her groceries. We left the store, and she turned to walk toward the bus stop. Before she left, I stopped her and said, "I want you to know why I helped you. I didn't help you because of your story. I helped you because I believe in God, and I believe the Bible is His Word. The Bible says that you're valuable because you're made in God's image. The Bible says that you have worth because Jesus was willing to die for you. And Jesus Himself said that we should give to the person who asks of us because Jesus Himself gave everything for us." With her eyes full of tears, she listened and simply said, "Thank you." Then, she walked away.

Do you know why I know what I said to that lady in such detail? Because it is what I say anytime someone asks me for money. "You are made in God's image. Jesus died for you. I am called to give to you without question." And do you know why I know what I say every time? Because God convicted the heck out of me about this several years ago, and I have approached the needy differently ever since.

In Matthew 5:42, Jesus says, "Give to the one who begs from you, and do not refuse the one who would borrow from you." Jesus is echoing a statement found throughout the Old Testament. As God's people, we have to give freely while expecting nothing in return. It is the kind of compassionate generosity Jesus showed us. We are expected to show it to others, especially those in need.

Many of you will take issue with me, and I understand your argument. You're hesitant to give to the needy because you can't be sure of what they are going to do with what you give. But I want to speak to you what the Lord spoke to me years ago: If a person in need takes your gift and spends it on alcohol or drugs, they are accountable to God for that decision. That's between God and them. But you are accountable to God for your heart. Do you take a posture of compassionate generosity when it comes to those in need? Are you openhanded? Do you give freely?

Jesus' entire ministry is full of expressions of compassion for those most in need. In the verse you read today, He clearly urges us not to resist a person in need. If we are going to be men who fill our culture with the compassion of God, we must make room to apply this compassion to those in our culture who are the most needy. By doing so, we are living, breathing expressions of the heart of God.

PROCESSING THE PURSUIT

1. Jesus obviously loves all people equally. But why do you think Jesus was so drawn to the poor, the outcast, and the sick? As a man seeking to pursue a Christ-centered masculinity, describe your attitude toward these same people. Does your attitude match up with Jesus' attitude?

2. What keeps you from being as generous to those in need as you could (or should) be? Don't just pass this question over. Stop and think about your response.

3. God has entrusted His message and ministry to you. That's part of what it means to be a Christ-follower. If we believe this, then we must believe that God uses us to accomplish His will. What if you saw every needy person as someone whom God had allowed to intersect with you just so that you might meet his or her needs in His name? What if you saw yourself as God's plan to show compassion to those in need? How would that change the way you engage with the poor and the outcast?

4. Many of you reading this don't struggle in this area. If this describes you, say a prayer thanking God for this fruit in your life. Ask Him to continue to help you grow in this area. Others reading this will say that, for whatever reason, this is an area in which you still must grow. Say a prayer today. Ask God to convict you of any un-Christlike attitudes you may have toward the "least of these." Ask Him to begin to grow in you a heart for the needy and a desire to be a messenger of God's compassion.

COMPASSION DAY 4

"FOR WE DO NOT HAVE A HIGH PRIEST WHO IS UNABLE TO SYMPATHIZE WITH OUR WEAKNESSES, BUT ONE WHO IN EVERY RESPECT HAS BEEN TEMPTED AS WE ARE, YET WITHOUT SIN." – HEBREWS 4:15

My father-in-law is as dear to me as anyone in my life. A while back, he found himself needing radiation therapy for a cancerous tumor in his brain. While the procedure was successful, the side effects were devastating. In a matter of days, he went from being a robust, strong man to being bedridden. He lost much of the use of his left arm and leg. Suddenly, we found ourselves helping him in and out of bed, lifting him into the car, guiding him into the wheelchair, and so on. And while the side effects were soon reversed by a follow-up surgery (praise God), the time spent caring for my father-in-law in this way made a lasting impression on me.

One of the most powerful emotions from this time was the compassion shown to my father-in-law. The interesting thing is that this compassion wasn't a burden because we were so sympathetic to his situation. How I wish my sympathy and compassion were always so evenly distributed.

Stop and read Hebrews 4:14–16. Pay close attention to verse 15. Jesus, our "high priest," is compassionate to us in large part because He can sympathize with our spiritual and moral weaknesses. While He lived a sinless life on this earth, He experienced temptation just like we do. He knows what it feels like. He experienced physical and emotional weaknesses as well. Jesus was fully God and fully human. So we know He got tired. He most likely got sick. We know He experienced grief. Jesus understood the human condition. When Jesus looks at us, the author of Hebrews says He sees us with sympathy. And as a result, we can approach Jesus expecting mercy and compassion.

When I can step back and evaluate the times I have not been Christlike in my expression of compassion, it almost always comes back to a lack of sympathy. It was easy for me to sympathize with the physical weakness of my father-in-law and, thus, show love and compassion. I don't always do so great at responding with sympathy to the spiritual weakness of people in my life. When I cease to be sympathetic to their situation, it's impossible to show compassion.

The relational conflict we experience in our lives always goes back to sin, whether it's our sinfulness, the sinfulness of someone else, or both. The Lord sympathizes with our human condition and responds with compassion. Shouldn't we do the same when it comes to the human condition of the people in our lives?

PROCESSING THE PURSUIT

1. Let's be real. There are some people in our lives who are rightfully tough to show compassion to. It's OK to admit that. If you find that you have these people in your life, take a moment and write a couple of their names down. (Here's a tough love moment: if you find that you have a ton of these people in your life, it may be that you're the problem. Just tossing that out there.)

2. Sympathy is at the heart of compassion, and the foundation of sympathy is understanding. Now I want you to do something that may not come easy. I want you to write a sentence or two about each of these people. And I want you to start the sentence this way: "To be more sympathetic to _____, I must understand that he/she _____." What factors in that person's life cause him or her to be so difficult to show compassion to?

3. Here's the honest to goodness truth: God sees every single one of our flaws in full view. Think about every single way you fall short of God's stan-dards. Every sin. Every shortcoming. Every weakness. God sees them all. AND STILL, in His grace and mercy, He sent His Son to pay the penalty your sins rightfully earn for you, just so He might be in relationship with you. If that is the attitude God has taken with us in full view of all of our sins, what do you need to do to change your attitude to be sympathetic toward the dif-ficult people in your life? Think and pray about the answer to this question as you go throughout your day.

COMPASSION DAY 5

"AND WHEN THE LORD SAW HER, HE HAD COMPASSION ON HER AND SAID TO HER, "'DO NOT WEEP.'" – LUKE 7:13

I don't like seeing other people in the midst of an awkward situation. My face gets hot. I get nervous for them. I think half the time I get more anxious than they do. Those YouTube videos of national anthem singers flubbing their lines or falling off the stage while they're singing? I don't watch them. Too much for me. But I have a friend who is the exact opposite. He's never met an awkward moment he didn't love. He doesn't know what it means to be uncomfortable with someone else's discomfort.

As we wrap up our look at what it means to be men who imitate the compassion of Christ, I want to hang out for a moment on this idea of being comfortable with other people's discomfort. Can we just have a moment of transparency? It can get super uncomfortable when we encounter someone who is hurting. Engaging with someone who is dealing with a setback or a loss of some kind can leave us not knowing what to do or say. But if we want to be men who model a Christ-inspired brand of compassion, we better get comfortable with other people's pain.

We could choose any number of biblical examples to focus on. But let's look at one that is maybe less well known. Turn to Luke 7 and read verses 11-17. Here, Jesus did what He did on several other occasions. He showed us that He experienced sorrow and that He wasn't afraid of it. This is important. First, it's important that God Himself knows and empathizes with our sadness. Second, it's important because it shows that Jesus is moved by the tough times we go through.

If you take nothing else from this book, I hope you have grasped the concept that we must define manhood as following the pattern set by Christ's life and teachings. As difficult as it is, as men, we have to work to notice people who are hurting and do what we can to meet their needs. If we care one bit about Jesus and living as He lived, we must make this a part of who we are. The powerful thing about this is that by doing so, we bring God's hope and light into our dark world. We are messengers of the Gospel simply by acknowledging the struggles of others. And I don't know about you, but that's the kind of thing I want to be a part of.

PROCESSING THE PURSUIT

1. Why is it difficult for us to always know how to meet the needs of those who are hurting?

2. Has someone ever shown you compassion when you were hurting from a loss or a tough setback? What did the individual actually do to show you compassion? How did it make you feel?

3. Is there anyone hurting in your life right now? What practical thing can you do right now to show God's compassion to this person? What will it take for you to follow through and actually do it?

4. Pray that God would show you people who are hurting and that He would give you the strength and awareness to reach out to them. Pray that He would help you overcome the awkwardness that can admittedly be associated with this type of situation. Remember, you are Christ's representative in this world. Showing compassion to the hurting is one way you live out a Christ-centered masculinity.

INFLUENCE

It doesn't take much of anything to influence a situation. Have you ever been sitting at a football game and you happen to be next to the one fan of the opposite team sitting in your section? It doesn't matter how many like-minded people are sitting around you; you'll feel that guy's influence every time his team makes a big play. Ever eaten a dish that was a little too salty? The right amount of salt makes a meal delicious. Overdo it just a bit and it's virtually inedible. Try and go for a run with a tiny rock in your shoe. You can't do it. Why? The influence of that small rock is too much.

In other words, a little bit of influence goes a long way.

One of the key characteristics of a godly man is how he influences the world around him. Jesus was the Son of God. And so any comparisons to Him are a little tricky. He kind of has an unfair advantage when it comes to being a man. But it should still blow our minds that Jesus' ministry only lasted three years. Talk about influence! Those three years have shaped centuries.

Here's a truth that will run through our time together this week: Not everyone is a leader, but everyone has influence. Some of you influence scores of people. Some of you influence only a small number. Regardless, your life makes an impact. Very few of us are "influence neutral." Most of us either have a positive influence or a negative one. How you use your influence will determine if you're living for God or living for yourself.

As you spend the next five days considering the role influence has on being a godly man, listen to what the Spirit is telling you about your ability to impact the world around you.

INFLUENCE DAY 1

"HEAR, MY SON, YOUR FATHER'S INSTRUCTION, AND FORSAKE NOT YOUR MOTHER'S TEACHING, FOR THEY ARE A GRACEFUL GARLAND FOR YOUR HEAD AND PENDANTS FOR YOUR NECK." - PROVERBS 1:8-9

Years ago there was a study conducted on which member of the family had the most spiritual influence. If a sibling was the first person to come to faith in Christ, there was a 7% chance the family would follow in faith. If the wife and mother became a follower of Christ, there was a 23% chance the rest of the home would follow her lead. But if the father became a follower of Christ, there was a 93% chance his home would follow his lead. That, my brother, is influence!

Proverbs 1:8-9 quotes a father to his son: "Hear, my son, your father's instruction, and forsake not your mother's teaching, for they are a graceful garland for your head and pendants for your neck." No one can replace the influence you have with your family, both from a positive and a negative perspective (which is an important point to make). And a check of your influence starts with a close look at the state of your family.

Do your children always look to their mother first for spiritual guidance? Does you daughter seem to date idiots? Where did she learn what to look for in a man? Is your son serious about his faith? Will he make his spiritual health a priority for his family? I can tell you this with zero hesitation: if your children don't see you making the spiritual health of your home a priority, they most likely will not see it as a priority in theirs.

God drove this truth home for me not long after I submitted to the Lordship of Christ. I was the type of man who was last to get ready for worship on Sunday. God convicted me that my children thought that my wife was the one making worship a priority because she was the first one they saw on Sunday mornings. But one of the most influential ways I was able to impact their attitudes toward church was in them seeing me come to the door and get them up for worship.

God convicted me, and I made a very slight but very powerful change. It impacted the entire dynamic of our home on Sunday mornings. When my children saw their father make worship a priority, they bought in, and it became a priority with them too. Where do you stand when it comes to your spiritual influence in your home?

PROCESSING THE PURSUIT

1. Simply put, this is gut-check time for you. This is a moment where you have to decide if you will ignore this question or listen to it. It's up to you. Ready? Here it goes: What kind of influence do you have on your family? Are you a positive influence or a negative one? Be honest with yourself.

2. Are you satisfied with the way you answered the previous question? What do you feel when you think about the influence you have on your family?

3. Big question. You may need some time to think about this one. What changes do you need to make to either establish or ramp-up your influence in your home? How can you partner with your wife to be more of a presence in your home?

4. Spend some time in prayer with God. Ask Him to give you the wisdom and the energy necessary to be the influence only you can be to your family.

INFLUENCE DAY 2

"I HAVE FOUGHT THE GOOD FIGHT, I HAVE FINISHED THE RACE, I HAVE KEPT THE FAITH." - 2 TIMOTHY 4:7

Today I want to point our attention to two legendary figures, both of whom are named Paul. The first is Paul "Bear" Bryant, who is known as one of the greatest football coaches in college football history. There is no doubt that Coach Bryant had a positive influence on many men. Then there is the Apostle Paul. This Paul is clearly a hero of the faith. However, if you were to ask men—especially men in my home state of Alabama—which one of these two Pauls they would consider to be their hero, many would pick the football coach. Interesting . . .

In his book Bear Bryant on Leadership, Pat Williams wrote that on his deathbed, the coach told the attending nurse that he regretted not using his influence to point people to Jesus Christ. But when we look at the Apostle Paul's letter to Timothy, written near the very end of Paul's life, we see Paul say the following: "I have fought the good fight, I have finished the race, I have kept the faith. Henceforth there is laid up for me the crown of righteousness, which the Lord, the righteous judge, will award to me on that day, and not only to me but also to all who have loved his appearing" (2 Tim. 4:7-8). Which one of these two men set the best example of what our state of mind should be as we near the end of our life? Better yet, which one set the example for how we should live?

Now you may be saying, "but I don't have the same platform or influence they had." Let me tell you a story. My grandmother was a powerful woman of God. She was also a lunchroom lady. And I have met hundreds of people around Birmingham, Alabama, who told me that she led them to Jesus Christ. We idolize great coaches. And yet, the vast majority of them don't use their considerable influence for God's glory. Coach Bryant admitted that he didn't. And while he and many others like him are big deals on earth, with statues and stadiums carrying their name, in heaven my grandmother is a much bigger deal.

Three people, each no longer with us. Three different stories of how they used their influence. When your life is over, how will the story of how you used your influence read?

PROCESSING THE PURSUIT

1. Have you ever considered the concept of how effectively you steward the platform you have been given? How would you describe your commitment to making the most of the influence God has given you?

2. What's one of the most challenging things you have ever accomplished? In other words, what is something you have worked extremely hard to achieve? What did it feel like when you were on the other side? What emotions were you feeling when you actually accomplished the thing you set out to accomplish?

3. What is keeping you from seeing your life in the same way you see the "big" accomplishment you just mentioned? It seems like the Apostle Paul saw his life this way. What would change about your Kingdom-impact if you viewed making the most of your influence as a goal worth pursuing?

4. Spend some time in prayer today reflecting on what God has to show you in this area. Ask God to give you a passion for using your influence for the sake of the Gospel. Listen to what God is telling you about areas in your life that are keeping you from having the kind of influence He desires you to have.

INFLUENCE DAY 3

"AND JESUS CAME AND SAID TO THEM, 'ALL AUTHORITY IN HEAVEN AND ON EARTH HAS BEEN GIVEN TO ME. GO THEREFORE AND MAKE DISCIPLES OF ALL NATIONS, BAPTIZING THEM IN THE NAME OF THE FATHER AND OF THE SON AND OF THE HOLY SPIRIT, TEACHING THEM TO OBSERVE ALL THAT I HAVE COMMANDED YOU. AND BEHOLD, I AM WITH YOU ALWAYS, TO THE END OF THE AGE.'" - MATTHEW 28:18-20

One of the ways we consider what it means to be a man is how we use the influence we've earned in our respective walks of life. As a Christ-follower, one of the main ways we practice good stewardship of our influence is through sharing the Gospel message of Jesus.

Read Matthew 28:18-20. These words may be pretty familiar to you. But if an outsider were to observe the way in which you live, would they see the commission Jesus gave His followers actually being put into action in your life? Jesus is clearly stating that He has the authority to send us into the world to influence the world and advance His Kingdom into every corner of society. He goes even further and tells us that as He sends us, He also goes with us on the journey. This is not only comforting, but it also means that if we have submitted to Jesus' lordship, we carry His influence along the journey as well. That's pretty powerful stuff.

If you unpack the Great Commission, Jesus says that step one is to make disciples. Though this looks differently in different situations, making disciples essentially means that we should be able to teach and lead to maturity those around us. It means we lead people to become more devoted followers of Christ.

Can I ask you a tough question, you know, man to man? Do you have the grasp of Scripture and the strength of faith to disciple anyone? If you are a husband and father, are you discipling your wife and children? I had a fellow brother rock my world one day over lunch when he told me that if anyone else was discipling my child that they were a better father than me. Let that one sink in.

Jesus goes on to say that we are to teach our household, and ultimately all who He has placed in our arena of influence, to obey all that He has commanded us. I remember in the 1990s the little WWJD bracelets became very popular. For you young men who missed the fad, WWJD stood for "What Would Jesus Do?" I want to challenge you with a truth: it is impossible to do what Jesus would do if you don't know what He did.

Jesus wants to use us to influence the world for His sake. But before we can have any influence for the Kingdom of God, we must first be disciples ourselves. If we want to teach others to obey all that Jesus has commanded us, we must first learn and apply these commandments to our own life. Only then will our influence be most effective.

PROCESSING THE PURSUIT

1. How do you feel about the impact you've had in leading people to Christ? Is this an area in which you have been faithful? Is this an area in which you need to recommit your passion and energy?

2. Have you ever considered that God would be far more efficient in winning souls if we weren't involved in the process? Yet, the Church is God's primary way of advancing the Gospel. That means God is more concerned with your experience in leading someone to Christ than He is in efficiency. Why do you think that is? What are you missing out on by not sharing your faith?

3. What is your biggest barrier to sharing your faith? Be honest. Admit it to yourself and to God. Now, what can you and God do to remove or overcome this barrier? Don't pass over this question. Spend some time in prayer and reflection and focus on what needs to be done to work through the obstacles that keep you from being as effective as God desires you to be.

INFLUENCE DAY 4

"THEN HE SAID TO HIS DISCIPLES, 'THE HARVEST IS PLENTIFUL, BUT THE LA-BORERS ARE FEW; THEREFORE PRAY EARNESTLY TO THE LORD OF THE HAR-VEST TO SEND OUT LABORERS INTO HIS HARVEST.'" - MATTHEW 9:37-38

Imagine sitting in a room with people who claim to love football. What if less than half of them had ever attended, watched, or listened to at least one game? Common sense would tell you that most of these guys aren't really fans. How could they be? I mean, how can anyone who says they love football not attend, watch, or listen to at least one game?

A few years ago, LifeWay Research polled thousands of Christians about their habits when it came to sharing their faith. Of those polled, 80% replied that it was important. But 61% admitted to not having shared their faith in the last six months. This means that more than half of the people who claim to love Jesus have not had one single Gospel conversation with anyone. Kind of like saying you're a fan of football but never watching a game.

The amazing thing to me about this study and others like it is that Jesus told those of us who claim to love Him to prove it by obeying His commands. In John 14:23-24, Jesus says, "If anyone loves me, he will keep my word, and my Father will love him, and we will come to him and make our home with him. Whoever does not love me does not keep my words." And what did Jesus command us? Among many other things, His last words to His disciples were to "go therefore and make disciples of all nations" (Matt. 28:19).

If I say that I believe in and love Jesus but I don't follow His instructions, then I'm a hypocrite. I don't truly believe what I claim. The reason some Christians have followed through with this commandment is that they truly believe what Jesus meant. So what about the other folks? Jesus said that if we love Him, we'll obey His commands. He said only those who do the will of the Father will inherit the Kingdom of Heaven (Matt. 7:21). And He said that "the gate is narrow and the way is hard that leads to life, and those who find it are few" (Matt. 7:14).

The bottom line is that we must be people whose lives back up their stated be-lief. We have to obediently follow after God. There's no quicker way to squander your influence than by saying you believe something but not living that way.

PROCESSING THE PURSUIT

1. We share the Gospel in our words and through our actions. What do your actions say about your faith? Are your actions advancing your influence or shrinking it?

2. For some of you reading this, it hurts to frame your Gospel influence in terms of obedience, doesn't it? The wonderful thing about God's grace is that it rescues us from the punishment our sins deserve. But Jesus still has a pathway He desires His people to follow. That's where obedience comes in. Why does framing your faithfulness, or lack of faithfulness, in terms of obedience make some of us squirm a bit?

3. Who do you have in your life that can hold you accountable for using your influence for God's glory? Are you willing to reach out to that person today and ask them to hold you accountable for how committed you are to sharing the Gospel?

INFLUENCE DAY 5

"IF I SAY, 'I WILL NOT MENTION HIM, OR SPEAK ANY MORE IN HIS NAME,' THERE IS IN MY HEART AS IT WERE A BURNING FIRE SHUT UP IN MY BONES, AND I AM WEARY WITH HOLDING IT IN, AND I CANNOT." - JEREMIAH 20:9

The Bible is a lot of things. It's a history of God's interactions with us. It's full of teaching that we can apply in living godly lives. It's a narrative story of who God is and how much He loves us. But it's also an awesome place to go for inspiration as men. There are countless examples of men whose lives inspire and encourage us. They teach us how to be men.

One of my heroes from the Bible is Jeremiah. Jeremiah is a guy who understood what it meant to use his influence. And as much as anyone, he understood the burden of influence. I'm so convicted by verse 9 of Jeremiah chapter 20. Immediately before this verse, Jeremiah is experiencing persecution for speaking the Word of God. Jeremiah is faced with considering what it might be like if he were to simply keep quiet to avoid persecution. Be silent and have people like you? Or speak truth and have people react with hostility? Jeremiah's words in verse 9 show that being silent isn't an option.

Jeremiah speaks of the fire that is shut up in his bones at the thought of NOT sharing the truth the Lord has given him. He can't keep himself from speaking about God!

Here's a thought: what if we were to actually speak about the things that we're passionate about, the things of God, no matter the response of those who hear our words?

When someone is around us, do they hear us talking about Jesus Christ? We are usually pretty free in sharing the things that "burn in our bones." The question is, based on the words you say each week, what would people say burns in your bones? Your kids' athletic activities? Movies or TV shows? Your hobbies? These things are all fine things to be engaged in. But where is your heart? Who we really are and what we really care about are often revealed through our words.

Brother, let me strongly encourage you to never hold back speaking the truth about your faith. Who knows, you may very well be the person God has ordained to lead someone from death to life.

PROCESSING THE PURSUIT

1. Can you describe a time when someone's words held a significant amount of power or meaning for you in your life?

2. Can you recall a time when you felt like saying something about your faith but didn't? What impulses kept you from doing so? Looking back, was it worth it?

3. Imagine yourself as someone whose words held real sway. Someone who, when he spoke, people listened. Someone who could be counted on to say the right thing even when it was difficult. Now, write down the main thing in your life that is keeping you from being that person.

4. Go to the Lord in prayer today. Ask Him to help you overcome the things that keep you from being a man whose words carry power. Ask Him to give you a spirit of boldness when it comes to speaking about the things of God.

CLOSING

It's our sincere hope that you didn't merely enjoy this book, but that it helped you think about manhood differently. If it was successful in doing this, it wasn't because of anything we did. If this book led you to think differently about your life as a man, it is only because this book pointed you to Jesus.

If there is a concept in this book that doesn't flow out of the person of Christ, it's a mistake. We cannot become anything close to the men we're supposed to be unless we're unrelenting in our pursuit of Christ. That is our heartbeat. We pray that it is yours too.

Before we wrap up, we wanted to leave you with a two-part challenge. First, we want to challenge you to be relentless in your drive to live a Christ-centered masculinity. Our world is dying for men to live and lead like Christ. Do whatever you have to do to be that man. Second, don't do it alone. Bring others along with you, whether it's a younger guy, or just a guy young in his faith.

If we can ever help you or your organization in anyway, we're easy to find. Don't hesitate to let us hear from you.

God Bless,

Rick Burgess and Andy Blanks

END NOTES

INTEGRITY DAY 2
Newheiser, J. (2008). Opening up Proverbs (p. 17). Leominster: Day One Publications.

SURRENDER DAY 5
Thomas, R. L. (1998). New American Standard Hebrew-Aramaic and Greek dictionaries: updated edition. Anaheim: Foundation Publications, Inc.

PASSION INTRODUCTION
Merriam-Webster, I. (2003). Merriam-Webster's collegiate dictionary. (Eleventh ed.). Springfield, MA: Merriam-Webster, Inc.

PASSION DAY 2
The Holy Bible: English Standard Version. (2016). Wheaton: Standard Bible Society.

PASSION DAY 5
Jamieson, R., Fausset, A. R., & Brown, D. (1997). Commentary Critical and Explanatory on the Whole Bible (Jn 10:10). Oak Harbor, WA: Logos Research Systems, Inc.

Robertson, A. T. (1933). Word Pictures in the New Testament (Jn 10:10). Nashville, TN: Broadman Press.

COMPASSION DAY 1
Platt, D. (2013). The Cross and Christian Suffering. In David Platt Sermon Archive (p. 4121). Birmingham, AL: David Platt.

ABOUT THE AUTHORS

RICK BURGESS

Rick Burgess is the Co-Host of the nationally syndicated Rick and Bubba Show. He has co-authored multiple New York Times Bestselling Books covering topics such as politics, marriage, business, comedy, and what it looks like to be a follower of Christ in secular entertainment. Rick has appeared on the Fox News programs Hannity's America, Your World with Neil Cavuto, and Fox and Friends.

Rick speaks regularly at men's events and marriage conferences across the country, all while teaching youth and men's Bible studies on a weekly basis. Rick is married to the former Sherri Bodine, and they have five children: Brandi, Blake, Brooks, Brody, and Bronner. Rick's wife Sherri is the author of the book "Bronner: A Journey to Understand," a powerful story about what she and Rick learned about God through the earthly death of their youngest son, Bronner. Rick's eulogy for Bronner became the most-viewed video in the world on YouTube the week of the service.

ANDY BLANKS

Andy Blanks is the Co-Founder of Iron Hill Press and YM360. A former Marine, Andy has been doing ministry since the early 2000s, having led the development of some of the most popular Bible study curriculum and discipleship resources in the country. He is an author, speaker, and podcast host who has been communicating the transformational power of God's Word for over two decades. He is passionate about helping people grasp God's call to live with purpose and meaning, spending their lives well for the sake of the Gospel. Andy has authored countless books, Bible studies, and articles and is a sought-after speaker. He also co-hosts a weekly podcast with his wife, Brendt.

Andy and Brendt were married in 2000 and have lived in Birmingham, AL, ever since. They have four children, three girls, and one boy.

CHALLENGE A YOUNG MAN IN YOUR LIFE TO PURSUE CHRIST-LIKE MASCULINITY

Do you want to take your son, or a small-group of teenagers, through the same challenging content as you experienced in *How To Be A Man*? Now you can. The *How To Be A Man: Student Edition* follows the same daily devotions as the adult version, but it's written just for young people. It's a powerful way to walk with a younger man (or younger men) through the journey of becoming the man God has called him to be.

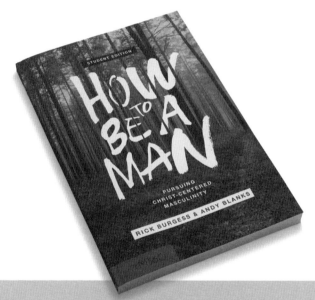

Because we want to help you be as effective as possible in walking young men through this book, we've provided you with a free study guide. We call it the "How To Be A Man Challenge."

TO ORDER YOUR STUDENT EDITION AND DOWNLOAD YOUR "HOW TO BE A MAN CHALLENGE," SIMPLY GO TO

HOWTOBEAMANCHALLENGE.COM

DOWNLOAD THE GUIDE FOR FATHER/SON, OR LEADER/TEENAGE SMALL GROUP. IT WILL EQUIP YOU TO OFFER AN EVEN GREATER CHALLENGE TO A YOUNG MAN TO IMPLEMENT WHAT HE'S LEARNING.

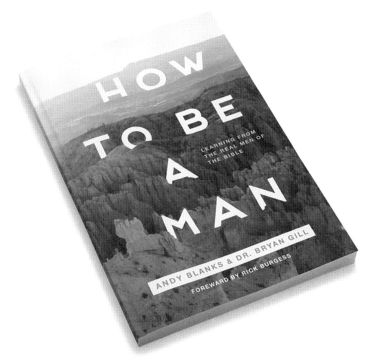

IRON HILL

press

Iron Hill Press is a collective of people who love Jesus, love Gospel truth, and love sharing those things with others through the medium of publishing and gospel-centered event experiences. Learn more about us at ironhillpress.com.

ironhillpress.com   888.969.6360